To Sharon,
Thank you for
your support
John Wheat

Sugar Coated War

John Breardon

Bloomington, IN Milton Keynes, UK
authorHOUSE®

AuthorHouse™
1663 Liberty Drive, Suite 200
Bloomington, IN 47403
www.authorhouse.com
Phone: 1-800-839-8640

AuthorHouse™ UK Ltd.
500 Avebury Boulevard
Central Milton Keynes, MK9 2BE
www.authorhouse.co.uk
Phone: 08001974150

This book is a work of fiction. People, places, events, and situations are the product of the author's imagination. Any resemblance to actual persons, living or dead, or historical events, is purely coincidental.

© 2006 John Breardon. All rights reserved.

No part of this book may be reproduced, stored in a retrieval system, or transmitted by any means without the written permission of the author.

First published by AuthorHouse 10/23/2006

ISBN: 1-4259-4807-3 (sc)
ISBN: 1-4259-6946-1 (dj)

Printed in the United States of America
Bloomington, Indiana

This book is printed on acid-free paper.

Please visit www.sugarcoatedwar.com

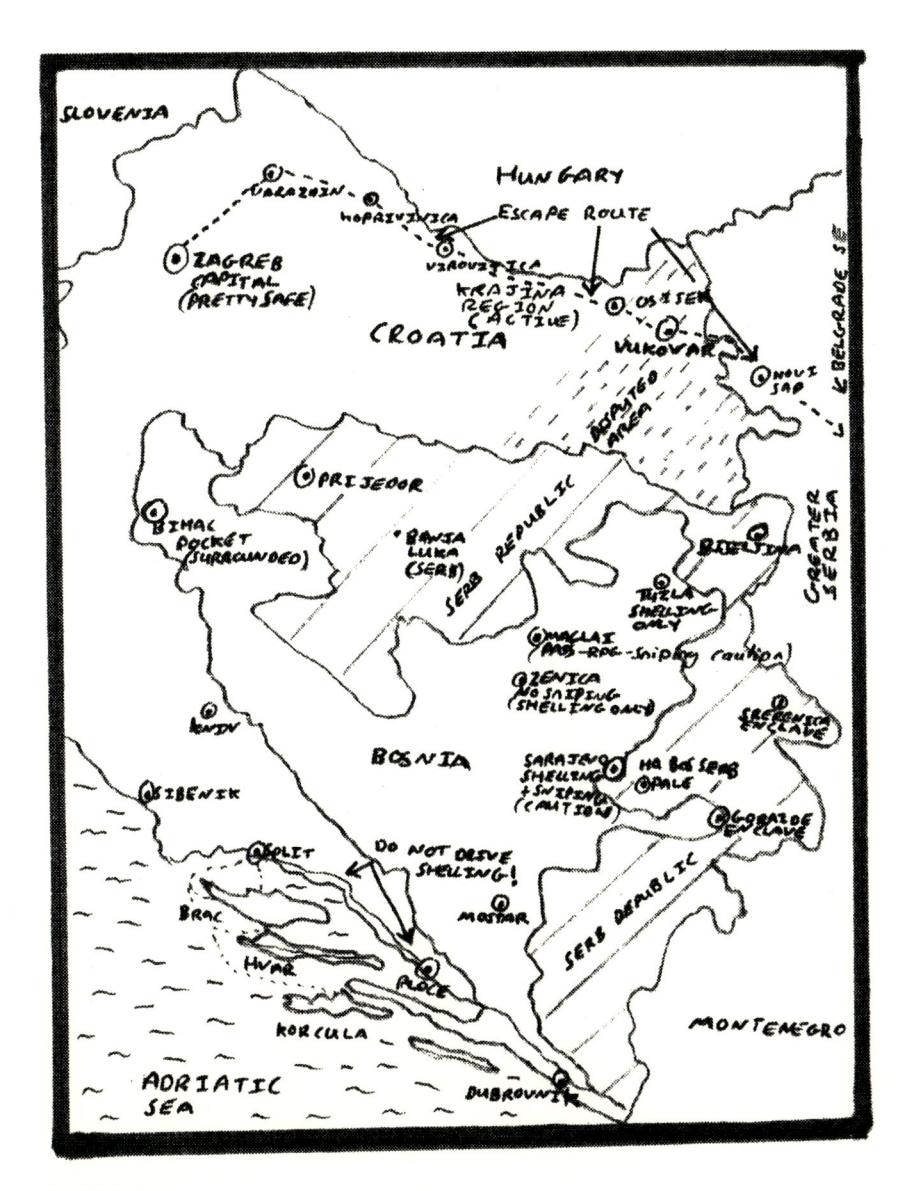

Field Map

Dedicated to Paul Goodall

Colleague and friend

Acknowledgment

In acknowledgement of all those who assisted in the production of this book.

Disclaimer

This book is largely a work of fiction. By its very nature it contains statements, which the author may not have been able to check or verify. The events and personal experiences described in this book represent a broad cross section of incidents that could, or in fact did take place, but may not necessarily be true as read.

It should also be noted that all the international relief organisations that the author encountered, strived to remain impartial throughout the conflict, and that the script is not representative, or indicative of relief workers in general, or any aid organisation. The characters with whom the author worked with should also be considered fictitious.

The book does not in any way seek to defame any organisation, or person contained herein.

'Shell them 'til the edge of madness'
Bosnian Serb' Army Commander
Sarajevo
1991

Foreword

The following political and military overview, is written for the benefit of those wishing to have a greater understanding of the complex circumstances, leading up to the fall of Yugoslavia...

The fall of the Berlin Wall, in November 1989, heralded a new era in Eastern Europe.

With the end of the Cold War, foreign aid to the liberalist Yugoslavia plummeted and the economy collapsed. Western governments no longer feared losing influence with the governing body and cut economic aid supporting the reputedly corrupt and inefficient Yugoslavian economy. There was now no threat of the Soviet Union extending its grasp any further towards a free and democratic Western Europe. Yugoslavia was out on its own; stuck between two ideologically conflicting regimes...

Josip Broz Tito emerged from obscurity and into the global spotlight in 1945. He had previously lead communist partisans against both the German occupation of Yugoslavia - and in the fight to depose the royal family of Yugoslavia in World War II. When the king of Yugoslavia was successfully deposed in 1943, Tito effectively became leader, albeit one of an occupied country. At the end of the war, and after liberation by the Russians, Yugoslavia was in ruins, with more than one-tenth of her population dead. A considerable number of these deaths had occurred as a result of massacres committed by Croatian fascists 'Ustaše', who supported and collaborated with Nazi Germany's occupation; killing many Serbian peasants and Royalist 'Chetnicks' (former Yugoslav soldiers with whom Tito's communist forces had been fighting at the same time as he fought the Germans). The seeds of dissent had already long been sown.

In 1946, after the close of World War II, Tito devised a new communist constitution, modelled on that of the Former Soviet Union. This foundation helped him facilitate his 'iron-fist' rule, over the Federal Republic of Yugoslavia for the next thirty-five years. He effectively suppressed any discontent amongst his people with his policy of brotherhood and unity, earning him both respect and fear - thus keeping Yugoslavia at peace.

Marshal Tito died on 4th May 1980 aged eighty-eight.

Ten years after his death, religious fanaticism exploded and flourished, as Yugoslavia was set alight. On the announcement of the death of Tito, the Former Yugoslavia lost its greatest and most potent symbol of unity - Tito.

The Former Yugoslavia consisted of six republics, Serbia, the largest, Bosnia-Herzegovina, Croatia, Slovenia, Montenegro, and Macedonia. Slovenia partitioned relatively peacefully. Macedonia and Montenegro remain, to this day, autonomous states within the Yugoslav Federation. However, there are a growing number of people in Montenegro who want independence. I expect in due course Montenegro will become a completely independent state.

Franjo Tudjman was voted into power as Croatia's new nationalist President in April 1990. The first parliament of the newly formed government, sat soon after on May 30th. This did not sit comfortably with people of Serbian origin living in Croatia. They had not forgotten the last time a nationalist leader was in power, some sixty years before - and the hundreds of thousands of Serbs - slaughtered at the hands of the Ustaše and Croat authorities in World War II. The Serbs feared persecution, now that a Nationalist was once again in power. Genuinely believing there was a threat, heavily populated Serbian areas in Croatia quickly united, and overwhelmed local Croatian Defence forces, confiscating their weapons. Other

Serbs simply packed all the belongings they could carry and headed eastwards - towards Serbia.

On 25th June 1991, following months of talks between the six republics, Croatia nervously declared its independence, fearing the powerful Serb Army located nearby would crush them. Fortunately for the Croats the Serbs did not attack, as the fledgling Croatian Army would have almost certainly crumbled. The European Community recognised Croatia's self-proclaimed status, in December 1991. This was despite any agreement, or apparent regard, for the protection of the peaceful ethnic Serb population, living in Croatia, at that time.

Meanwhile, President Slobodon Milošević, the Communist Serbian Leader, previously voted into office in December 1990, quietly stoked the flames of unrest in Croatia. He soon provided substantial military support for the Serbian cause in Croatia.

A proclamation of independence by Bosnia, under Alija Izetbegović, quickly followed. Izetbegović, refused to allow Bosnia to be carved up by President Franjo Tudjman of Croatia, and President Slobodon Milošević of Serbia. Despite Serbian reservations about Croatia declaring independence, the carving up of Bosnian territory for themselves, was something they both had very much in common. With this desire, the death sentence on the Former Yugoslavia was finally passed.

It is important not to forget Slovenia, who had also declared her independence on the same day as Croatia: somewhat more boldly than the Croats. They immediately kicked out the Yugoslav customs officials from their borders with Italy and Austria. Consequently, on the 27th June 1991, a stand off occurred with the Yugoslav (Serb) Army, who sent some two thousand five hundred troops to retake the border posts but not 'invade' Slovenia. Slovenia, immediately mobilised her own thirty five thousand troops and police, surrounding the 'invaders', and trapping remaining Serbian troops in their Slovenian barracks.

In spite of warnings, the Serbs flew a helicopter over Ljubljana, the Slovenian capital. The Slovenians promptly shot it down. Ironically, the helicopter was carrying bread to the beleaguered Yugoslav troops, piloted by a Slovenian serving with the Yugoslavians.

By now, both Croatia and Slovenia were engaged in a low-key war with Yugoslavia. Reluctantly, the Yugoslavian authorities, agreed to the separation of Slovenia from Yugoslavia, and promptly withdrew its army on July 18th, the rhetoric being that they had no territorial claim to the land as it was 'ethnically pure', containing no significant Serbian population. The reality was that Serb Army Intelligence had warned their politicians that, despite the size of the Yugoslav Army, it would be substantially overstretched fighting both Slovenia and Croatia. Not fighting Slovenia would allow the Yugoslav Army to focus its attention on Croatia, where some six hundred thousand Serbs lived.

In response to the perceived threat, the predominately Serbian populated towns in Croatia, had begun to expel all Croatian and non-Serbian inhabitants. Their intention was to form a Serb mini-state 'Republika Srbska', and then somehow link up with Greater Serbia.

Vukovar, an eastern Croatian town bordering Serbia, heavily populated by Serbs, was extremely vulnerable to unrest. In May 1991, the Croatian police confidently drove down the high street to dismantle a Serbian roadblock. They were ambushed by local Serbian paramilitaries, resulting in the deaths of twelve Croat policemen. A further twenty-two were wounded. This infuriated the Croat masses resulting in Croatia mobilising all her reservist forces in the eastern provinces - bordering Serbian territory. The Serbian response was to send a 'peacekeeping' force, supposedly to 'stabilise' the situation, and protect the Serbian population. In reality, Serbian tanks and infantry swept through town after town in eastern Croatia, killing, without mercy and in abundance, any Croatians who had not fled. The Croats defending Vukovar, who had already reputedly destroyed many Serbian homes, were massacred. War, yet again, had taken a firm grip of this proud nation.

In September 1991, in an effort to stop any further slaughter, the leaders of all six of the Yugoslav Republics attended a European Community convention, whereupon the United Nations (UN), fearing all out war, imposed an arms embargo on all the Former Yugoslavia. Milošević, argued that if Croatia had the right to independence, then so should Serbian people living in Croatia. Despite some promising gestures and intentions from all sides, the talks proved fruitless and soon failed. The arms embargo left Bosnia at a serious disadvantage, as she had little in the terms of military hardware. Although better off, Croatia could not match Serbia militarily.

April 1992, with her army fully mobilised, the Serbs set their eyes on another target - Bosnia, which was inhabited by half a million Serbs - a third of the entire population of Bosnia.

Serbian soldiers first took the strategic North-Eastern Bosnian town of Bijeljina - a major crossroads linking Bosnia and Serbia. Unfortunately, for the Serbs, a civilian photographer documented atrocities committed by 'less discerning' Serbian troops. Once publicised, these photographs caused outrage in Bosnia, and in particular, amongst the more cosmopolitan and sophisticated people of Sarajevo.

Terror, rape, persecution, and death, was commonplace in Bosnian Muslim towns taken by Serb forces. Those not killed or sent to 'concentration camps' were expelled with nothing more than they could carry. This became routine practice. In the 'blitzkrieg' that followed, the Serbs rapidly sliced through Bosnia, and in doing so took control of three quarters of this ill prepared, and largely undefended state.

In time, the Serbs would learn what western powers had learned from the war in Vietnam. Keep the press at bay and their cameras out. The sight of death and destruction on television can have a damaging effect on any war effort. These measures went some way to hide the many atrocities that took place. Atrocities, that soon became a trademark of this war, hidden - at least for the time being.

In April 1992, Bosnian Serb forces backed by Serbia began sporadic sniping and shelling against Sarajevo, the Bosnian capital. A major offensive was soon to follow. Serbian forces from the southwest, southeast and northwest, launched a simultaneous, three-pronged attack, supported by Soviet built T62 main battle tanks and Mig 25 fighters, dropping a variety ordinance in a ground attack role, killing many innocent civilians.

All able-bodied men in Sarajevo were quickly called to arms. Alongside professional soldiers served civilian criminal gangs, police, and the remaining Serbs living in the city, who believed in a multi-cultural society. Serbian forces managed to get within fifty feet of the Bosnian Presidency Building. Bosnian street fighters, with a few

Rocket Propelled Grenades, sheer determination and guts, stopped the Serb tanks in their tracks. Some of the defenders climbed onto tanks, mercilessly pouring petrol through open hatches - burning the occupants alive. Many, getting themselves killed in the process.

Despite the brave acts of the defenders, the battle for Sarajevo was only just beginning, with the living conditions for the inhabitants of Sarajevo worsening daily.

The advantage clearly lay with those defending. The narrow streets of old Sarajevo provided excellent cover to ambush Serbian troops, in hard-hitting bloody and dogged encounters. This tactic ultimately turned the table on the attackers. Many Serbian troops, unfamiliar with the complex back streets of the city, became surrounded and trapped by local Bosnian Muslim forces. Some were captured - most summarily executed on the spot. The unlucky ones were brutally clubbed to death; such was the anger of the city's inhabitants.

On May 3rd 1992, Alija Itzabegović was returning from yet another peace conference held by the European Community in Lisbon, Portugal. Shortly after landing at Sarajevo Airport, he unfortunately fell into Serb hands. This was simply due to not meeting up with a planned United Nations escort that was supposed to usher him to safety (a UN contingent now occupied Sarajevo Airport). This could have been tragic to the Bosnian Muslim cause, but proved to be only a slight set back. Following negotiation, Itzabegović was exchanged for captured Serbian troops; thus allowing hostilities to continue, and each side claiming a small propaganda victory.

Peace efforts sponsored by European countries continued, but the Serbs cared little, and had by now virtually surrounded Sarajevo, in an attempt to cut it off from the rest of the world. They were now ready to finish off this bastion of Bosnian resistance. In December 1992, Lord Owen, Europe's peace negotiator, arrived in Sarajevo, bringing a clear message to the besieged Muslims.

'Don't, don't, don't live under this dream that the west is going to come in and sort this problem out. Don't dream dreams.'

Comments such as this were seen as a clear indication to the Serbs, that the West had little interest in events that were taking place, and seemingly gave them the green light to prosecute the war more vigorously - which they did. It was made quite clear to the Bosnian Muslims that they were going to be on their own - against the might of the reasonably well-equipped and well-trained Serbian Army.

The war intensified, with all ethnic divides fighting for what they considered a righteous cause. A war that was to be fought with a fundamental disregard for human life: a war that was to be remembered more by images than words.

Radovan Karadzić, the leader of the Bosnian Serbs, publicly announced that he was determined to gain control of sixty-five per cent of Bosnia, renaming it, The Serbian Republic of Bosnia Herzegovina. After the war, Karadzić said.

'If the United Nations deployed just ten thousand troops to block supply routes to the Bosnian Serb Army in the initial stages of the conflict, they would have been finished.'

As world condemnation grew, safe enclaves manned by United Nations soldiers were established, the first of these being in the town of Srebrnica. The Serbs initially agreed not to overrun the town, but insisted that the Bosnian Muslim forces disarm. The UN claimed this as a much-publicised victory but, in reality, it meant the Serbs could take the town at any time they wished and ultimately did. The few Canadian UN soldiers stationed there could do seldom little to stop them. The UN victory was indeed hollow, and nothing more than a face saving exercise for the press.

Goražde, another 'safe area' came under heavy shelling from Serbian artillery. General Rose, the British UN Commander responsible for the enclave, decided not only to deter further Serb action (as prescribed in the UN mandate at the time), but to deter it with the first ever NATO air strikes in the region, destroying a tent, that was the Serbian Command Headquarters. This in itself was not *all* that significant, but did indeed show that the West was prepared to use such force, albeit, at the time, in very small doses. The Serbian reaction was one of anger. They surrounded the one hundred fifty or so UN soldiers encamped in Goražde, vowing that none would leave Serbian territory alive. This was the first of many instances, where the tactical vulnerability of the UN troops would be exposed.

The United States government, who were becoming more vocal as atrocities were exposed, gave the Serb Commander an ultimatum. Allow the encircled troops freedom and discontinue the attack on Goražde, or else. No one really ever knew what the 'or else' actually meant: the United States was not particularly clear of its intentions (I am not sure they knew either). The Serbs did not act on threats from the usually impotent West and did not in any way fear them. However, they withdrew to their previous positions and allowed the UN troops to continue their mission, and for the moment, fulfil their mandate in their 'peacekeeping' role. The siege of Goražde carried on much as before. Žepže, another eastern Bosnian 'safe area', was soon overrun with vengeance. In the intervening time, some ten thousand civilians had already died in Sarajevo, from shelling, sniping, or quite simply defending their homes. All whilst the UN soldiers, under their current mandate, had no choice but to helplessly watch.

In July 1995, surviving Muslim soldiers, left alive in the Srebrnica area and tired of waiting for promised UN protection, mounted hit and run raids against the Serbs. Armed with little more than small arms, and the odd Rocket Propelled Grenade, they weren't terribly successful. However, the attacks helped relieve the frustration of being surrounded for almost three years. The raids also boosted their morale, and provided a glimmer of hope, to the completely impoverished and starving population of Srebrnica. Direct attacks on the Serbians, also gave the Bosnian Muslims an opportunity to avenge the deaths of their family and friends murdered in nearby woods. Any Serbian soldier captured by these irregular forces, was doomed to a very gruesome death at the hands of men, who had lost everything and genuinely felt that they had nothing to live for, except the act of unpitying vengeance. These attacks were more of an annoyance to Serbian forces than effective military action.

Srebrnica soon became home to thousands of refugees, who had managed to sneak through Serbian lines, from other overrun towns and villages that had succumb to the Serbian offensive. This put more strain on the very limited supplies of food.

There were no lines defining hostile territory. Any mountain pass, road or street could be mined or provide ideal terrain to ambush convoys of military vehicles, or humanitarian aid. Convoys quickly learned not to slow down when confronted with a small fire in the road ahead, but to expect a salvo of stones and rocks, aimed at the windscreens of their vehicles; thrown by disgruntled and misguided youths. This proved to be nothing more than an indication of what aid workers, press, and UN Peacekeepers could expect later, as hatred and disdain for all participants intensified in the Former Yugoslavia. Mortar teams targeted supply routes; abandoned houses harboured snipers, hostile towards anyone they suspected of interfering in their own, murderous, final solution.

I do not believe the war was one of an absolute ethnic nature, as popular media would have us believe, but one of a nationalist origin, with a religious and sometimes ethnic bias. It was certainly a war without pity. How could it be wholly ethnically based when the persecution of a whole population, *by* the population was perpetrated; irrespective of whether they were Serbians, Croatian Serbians, Bosnian Serbians, Croatian Muslims, or indeed, Croatians themselves. However, for the purpose and readability of the book I have often described the combatants by their ethnic group, irrespective of their geographical location, as each seemed to be engaged in their own territorial and ideological war within the war. Unlike the Nazi persecution of the Jews, the Former Yugoslavia tore itself apart from within.

All warring parties were guilty of the well-scripted atrocities that took place. All sides were persecutors and the persecuted. Nationalism, sponsored by religious fanaticism, facilitated by competing empires and ideologies over the centuries, had ingrained a strong nationalist identity amongst the people of this traditionally troubled region.

The death of Tito meant that the country was lacking in strong and consistent leadership that had previously controlled such nationalistic rivalry. All groups remained uncompromisingly true to their historic origins.

Was the war one of ethnic rivalry? A war of nationalist fervour perhaps? Or simply one of perceived historical territorial rights, or indeed a combination of all three. I, along with some of my colleagues who were also to risk their lives - and die - helping the victims of the war, did not have the answer. You - the reader - must decide...

This is my account of the conflict - where over four hundred thousand people died during four blood-drenched years of war...

Introduction

As a professional driver, employed by a local white goods manufacturer, I was given the choice of going onto the factory floor, or being made redundant. I took the first option and found myself on a production line. The prospect of working indoors was not one I was used to or indeed relished.

At that time, war was raging throughout Bosnia and the Former Yugoslavia. The television coverage was disturbing. I particularly remember scenes of Global Relief Organisation, and UN trucks winding their way through ice-capped mountains, towns, and villages, bringing much needed relief to a country savagely torn apart by war. I wanted to be there. I held a Class 1 Heavy Goods Vehicle Licence and had completed an army all terrain driving course. This coupled with other driving experience, and what I believed to be a mature approach to life was, I hoped, enough for me to be selected for service with one of the aid agencies operating in the region.

I approached the British Home Office with a view to working for the United Nations but, at that time, no one else was required. They recommended I try the Global Relief Organisation who responded similarly, but I was determined to 'do my bit'; for not only the suffering people of the Former Yugoslavia, but also to get out of the trap that I now felt I was in. I was desperate to do something with my life, to put myself 'on the map', so to speak. I continued to telephone the Global

Relief Organisation on a regular basis: my persistence eventually paid off.

Being selfish, I did not discuss my intensions with Paula my fiancée, who had recently moved in with me. This in fact typified my self-centred and determined attitude at that time.

The most profound and shocking experience of my life
This is my story

Amended Script

Preface

Memoirs of life on the ground of an aid worker.

My small part in contemporary European history began when I attended an Interview Board at The Global Relief Organisation office in London. The following week, after bring medically examined and inoculated I was declared fit for service: right time right place.

I was jubilant, excited, and just a little bit nervous, but most of all I welcomed the opportunity of leaving behind the prospect of what I felt was a mundane existence, working on a production line, along with the everyday monotony of being 'normal'; 'nine 'till five an' all that'. At last! A chance to break away from complying with the low expectations expected of me. An opportunity to show my parents, that I was not as worthless as I had felt as a teenager and whilst growing up.

I wasted no time in telling the personnel department that I was leaving. Most people working on the same production line as I wished me well, and asked me to keep in touch. I said I would but never did.

In March 1993, I flew to Brussels, Belgium, and underwent a few days' induction, in order to give me some idea of what to expect. My conception of war was incomplete and naively limited.

I was soon to realise that nothing can prepare someone for the emotional experience of war, apart from the bitter experience itself. I undertook the venture with an innocence, which was destined to be lost forever…

After leaving Belgium, I flew to Vienna, then onto Zagreb, the capital of Croatia.

Looking out of the windows from the twin engined Fokker 50, a small, twenty-seat aircraft, full of United Nations Officers and news reporters, Croatia appeared quite normal. The war had not at that time, affected large parts of the country.

I noticed the odd convoy of white aid trucks snaking their way over the meandering, mountainous roads, and wondered if I would be travelling along those very same roads. On arrival at Zagreb Airport, I was met by an English speaking, locally employed Global Relief Organisation driver, and driven to the nearby Headquarters and introduced to a number of my new colleagues. I spent the next few days undergoing many briefings and familiarising myself with the staff, equipment, and vehicles, whilst it was being decided where I would be deployed.

My first deployment was in Split, on the Adriatic Coast in Croatia. At that time, a bitter and protracted dispute was taking place between the convoy drivers already deployed, and the Global Relief Organisation who, in the safety and comfort of their Headquarters in Brussels, refused to budge on the matter of providing protective clothing for their workers.

The drivers were on strike and vehemently refused to participate in any more relief convoys until issued with flak-jackets and helmets. A few trucks had been badly hit by shrapnel on a recent convoy, and they were genuinely fearful. The Global Relief Organisation held the view that the sanctity of the Global Relief Organisation insignia would protect them; this may have been true sixty years ago, but it did not seem to be working now. In actual fact, the Global Relief Organisation insignia, I soon learned, was often used as target practice, much to the amusement of the warring parties. The logo often proved to be totally ineffective in this war, shattering the notion that the Global Relief Organisation and other relief organisations were inviolable.

A convoy had already been ambushed early on in the war, whilst en-route to Sarajevo, the convoy leader killed and all five drivers injured.

A video shot after the event, was shown to all new drivers, and proved to be as thought provoking as it was harrowing. It initially left an impression upon me, but I soon managed to brush aside the scenes of shot up Global Relief Organisation vehicles, in the belief that it would never happen to me. I was young, and my faith in my immortality remained resolutely intact. Casualties and death were something that you read about in the newspaper, or listened to on the radio - it could never happen to me. The Global Relief Organisation wanted to preserve its image of being of a non-aligned status - and impartial. They felt that flak-jackets and helmets would present a military image. To a degree, I think they were right.

Following long-drawn-out debate, and with the possibility of the whole relief effort grinding to a halt; the demands of the drivers were met. This was only after much deliberation and consternation by senior staff in Brussels.

Two days later the requested protective equipment arrived, and promptly issued to the drivers, enabling the relief effort to resume.

I spent my first eight months living in Split, on the Dalmatian Coast, which was quite beautiful. I made two or three day trips to besieged enclaves throughout Bosnia. There were four or five ten ton trucks on a typical convoy, plus a convoy leader and a field officer, who was a local employee and knew the terrain, language and equally importantly the local customs. The addition of a locally employed field officer was only possible if no confrontation lines were to be crossed. The civilian field officer stood the risk of and had on at least one occasion, been taken prisoner when crossing into his 'enemies' territory - only to be released after determined negotiation by Global Relief Organisation officials. This was despite having a Global Relief Organisation identity card. The trips usually lasted two or three days and were sometimes hazardous, but life in Split itself was generally good. On reflection, I shall remember it as one of the most enjoyable and rewarding times of my life. The war hadn't really affected this prosperous town. Yes, inflation was high and cigarettes, a national pastime, were expensive, but there was plenty of good food and drink available. A clash between a holiday and a drama.

The Global Relief Organisation had hired a number of holiday apartment blocks situated right on the coast. I had my own flat, which had a small kitchen, bathroom, bedroom, and a small balcony overlooking the Adriatic Sea. The accommodation was excellent and not what I had expected, after all, I was in a 'war zone' and here to help the victims of war and endure a 'warlike' existence.

In the same accommodation block was a twenty-seven year old Frenchman named Vince. Nearby was Richard, aged thirty from Scotland, and Timmy, aged forty, from England: we soon became good friends. Vince was great fun to be around and we would often find ourselves taunting Richard (the sensible one) for nothing more than being so sensible!

Vince had been a trucker back in Belgium, but was tired of working the long hours he was forced to work. This was much the same for truckers worldwide with twelve hours a day being typical. As a way of relaxing from the tension of driving through war zones, we were determined to have as much of a carefree and irresponsible time as possible - whilst not on convoy. Apart from trusty and reliable Richard that is.

Richard was a very likeable, level-headed, and usually a much-reserved man. He had a wife and two children and prior to working for the Global Relief Organisation had his own haulage business, operating three trucks. Alas, as with so many small businesses, the crippling wait between providing a service, and being paid, forced him into liquidation. On one occasion, he waited eighteen months for payment, but six months was more typical. He was determined to make good his loss and now ten years on he is successfully running two businesses.

Richard's rooms were directly above Vince's. Vince and I would stay up late and gently tap the end of a broom handle on the ceiling above, taking turns in ten-minute stints. To our amusement, this drove Richard to absolute despair and, on one occasion, when Vince had unofficially 'borrowed' a Land Rover from headquarters, Richard, in the dead of night, got up, and removed all the wheels, hiding them in various locations around the apartment gardens. I thought this was really funny, until the local headquarters wanted to know which one of us 'vagrants' had stolen the Land Rover. Vince admitted to his crime but, when asked to bring it back, had to tell them that he couldn't bring it back because it hadn't any wheels, saying that he thought someone was playing a practical joke. Richard was the one playing the practical joke. Removing and hiding the Land Rover wheels was, I thought, a little out of character. He would not reveal where the wheels were until we guaranteed to stop tormenting him. This we reluctantly did, albeit temporarily. The temptation of torment proved too much and Richard continued to be plagued by our antics throughout the summer of '93.

Burt, a balding 'old man' of about fifty years of age, a longstanding trucker, would shamefully join Vince and me in some of our roguish activities. He was very easily led, and obviously enjoying a second youth. I remember one night how we took great delight in getting him drunk, to the point where he could barely stand. We sat him on the floor leaning against a wall, and howling with uncontrolled laughter, cut tufts of grey hair from one side of his head, super-glued it across his forehead, and gave him a 'neat' new fringe to the mumblings of

'What you bastards doin'?' whilst falling to his side and passing out.

'Aussie' Pete was twenty-seven, the same age as myself, and had spent most of his life drifting around Australia, and the world; putting his mechanical and driving skills to use whenever he wanted a job. With his amazing sense of black humour, he would keep us permanently amused with his constant stream of witticisms. Another Australian, John Corbin, was a twenty-eight year old marine mechanic and truck driver, living a similar lifestyle to Pete. He also became a close member of the team.

'Timmy Tubby' (the original Teletubby because he was somewhat overweight) was a committed trucker. I expect the monotony of travelling up and down the motorways of Britain, eating a high cholesterol diet, had not only taken its toll on his waistline, but also his mental state. He was a thoughtful man and always willing to help, obviously enjoying his new found role, taking the job more seriously than most of us; he would often come up with ideas to improve efficiency and 'quality of service': all to no avail. We were having a good time and no one was going to spoil it! The seven of us made a formidable team. Always in competition with the German contingent, who lived in a much plusher apartment than ours, further up the coast.

To let off steam, raiding parties using small rowing boats would 'attack' the Germans' apartment with the primary goal to steal food and take a prisoner (the Germans had much better food at their apartment). There would be a brief melee if detected - sometimes we had to walk back if the Germans seized our boats. Any prisoners we took were tied to the pier next to our apartment, in water up to their chests whilst the tide gently rose… If the other Germans heard the victim's pleas, he would be exchanged for some of their excellent food!

Headquarters soon learned of our activities and threatened to split us up into different apartments, or even send us home if our 'laddish' antics didn't cease. They *needed* us… and we knew it: we took little notice.

In stark contrast with the miserable experience of adolescence, I was finally enjoying my 'teenage years', very late in coming and quickly settled into life in Split. This was in spite of our convoys going to some of the worst parts of Bosnia; it was, for the most part, quite simply wonderful…

Split was an ancient trading port, now flourishing with a new and unexpected trade - the smuggling of illegal arms. Clearly in contravention of the United Nations arms embargo, imposed on the region. The harbour was awash with large luxury yachts, many bringing in arms to beleaguered Croatia from Italy. One of many ways the Croats were re-arming their ill-equipped forces. Other weapons, of East European origin (mainly the former East German Army), were reputedly donated by the German government and smuggled in by road. The Bosnians weren't able to re-arm so easily, and ultimately came to rely on arms smuggled from other illegal western sources - the United States believed to be one such source.

On days of inactivity, we would meet on the beach in front of our apartment early in the morning, then swim some half mile up the coast, working up an appetite for breakfast. Shortly after, we would usually catch a taxi into town.

Split was as fascinating as it was beautiful. Built in 295 AD by the Roman Emperor, Diocletion, the ancient centre and surrounding area was the same as when originally built - making it quite unique. Purpose built holes carved into the thick palace walls housed sandwich bars.

Restaurants with tables and chairs outside were squeezed into cool dark passages, sheltering diners from the sun. The pathways were worn away by 1,700 years of the hustle and bustle of traders and shoppers alike.

The Black Market was thriving, particularly in the exchange of money. This was a direct result of inflation running at around 20% per day. Deutchemarks, the preferred currency, was much sought after. My living allowance was paid in Deutchemarks and the exchange rate on the Black Market could easily be 30% more than the bank rate. Consequently, local currency was obtained pretty much on a daily basis, via the seedy Black Market back streets. We would never go alone to exchange money, preferring safety in numbers to conduct any shady deals...

Evenings were usually spent seeking out one of the many coastal restaurants that had previously thrived with the influx of tourism before the war. After dinner, a casino, or disco in one of the nearby hotels, (now housing refugees from Bosnia) would be a favourite venue to spend the evening.

We sometimes faced hostility from local people, partly because we had money to spend and partly because we represented countries that the refugees blamed for not helping them enough in their current demise. Tension amongst the refugees was always high. On one occasion, a pistol was fired in the disco and a man killed, during disputes between the angry and cramped refugees.

Each morning, in the nearby army base, the United Nations would hold a security and press briefing, disclosing details of any security incidents and developments that had taken place, over the last twenty-four hours. This also included the demeanour of the local populace and any acts of aggression towards United Nations workers. 'UN Govno' ('UN Shit') or UN Mafia, was painted in large letters on walls by unhappy locals.

Although it was in my interests to attend such briefings, I never did. After all, I wasn't there to be killed, so why should I bother? I would rather spend my time on the beach, with the others; or fishing on the apartment owner's boat. Life was indeed good.

A patchwork of confrontation lines would be crossed several times during a trip; all needing appropriate paperwork. However, despite having the correct documentation, soldiers at checkpoints were often reluctant to allow us to pass, believing our supplies would end up in the hands of their enemies, something that the Global Relief Organisation made great effort to avoid. These checkpoints, were either manned by very professional soldiers or drunken youths, who would often brandish their guns in a menacing manner. Consistency in the professionalism of troops was to be something that I learned was not to be taken for granted in this war; making it difficult to maintain a friendly, positive approach at some checkpoints. War trophies, such as unborn babies, ripped from the wombs of pregnant women, and pickled in large glass containers, resembling large jam jars (a common occurrence whereby the victim was ordered to choose the knife that would be used to mutilate her) and corpses hanging from telegraph masts were displayed nearby.

These scenes were disturbing, but somehow, looking at them from inside my lorry cab, I felt quite removed and not, at that time, terribly concerned. I had mentally prepared myself for such scenes of horror, but did in fact initially find it quite mesmerizing. There was nothing I could do; anyway, I was having a good time. That was what happened in war - wasn't it?

European Monitors, who were civilian personnel and dressed in white, were commonly known as 'cricket-bats' as opposed to 'britbats' - British Battalion United Nations troops, 'spanbats' - Spanish Battalion, etc. They would roam the country at will, putting themselves at great risk in an effort to ensure the war was fought in an 'honourable - clean manner', as they would say when chatting at a bar. Despite what politicians tell us, and after my own experience, I don't think any war can ever be honourable or clean. In actual fact, all sides saw them as irritants, none more so than the predominately Serbian Yugoslavian National Army (JNA). They had a deep resentment of these white clinical figures, which were reputedly nearly all Western Intelligence Officers who wandered, with an assumed impunity, across the disputed territories of the Former Yugoslavia. Four were killed, when a Yugoslav jet shot down one of their helicopters and another killed, whilst on duty in the town of Mostar, quite early on in the war. This event was an early illustration of the hostility the international community faced throughout the whole of the war.

Nonetheless, the presence of the monitors and their recording of events undoubtedly saved many innocent people, who would have otherwise been slaughtered.

This was a conflict where neighbour fought neighbour, barely a family had not been affected by the war and its destruction. Many Serbs had married Muslims and their loyalties were split between both their old and new families. Indeed, some sixty thousand blameless Bosnian Serbs had not fled their homes. Many still lived in the besieged city of Sarajevo, whose inhabitants were predominantly Bosnian Muslims and mostly tolerant of the minority Serbian population. Serbs, living in surrounding districts, maintained the view that they were either hostages or collaborators. In other besieged enclaves, towns and villages, the ethnic minority was not so readily accepted, resulting in the massacre of many innocent civilians.

At times, it was difficult to remain unbiased, and not take sides with the weak against the strong, and to maintain an affinity with victims from all sides caught up in the nauseating barbarism of the Balkan War. Some would argue that such neutrality does not exist in the face of murder, and that doing nothing to stop it - *is* in fact taking sides.

On reflection, I don't think I was ever entirely neutral, rightly or wrongly seeing the Serbs as the aggressor, but it is fair to say I met and had close association with many good, honest Serbian people, as much as I did Bosnians and Croats.

Despite professional military leadership, the influence of the United Nations did not solve the issues of the war, barely managing to oversee the dialogue that would lead to numerous, completely ineffective ceasefires. Peace did not come to the Former Yugoslavia until effective intervention by the United States some years later.

Chapter One

We stopped for a break prior to driving a steep mountain ascent. I opened one of my German Army ration packs and, after the usual exchange of banter and trading of unwanted items, began to eat whilst walking over to a nearby skip to lean against. As I approached, a gentle prevailing breeze wafted the most sickening, gut churning smell I had ever encountered. Heaving, wanting to be sick, fascination took a hold of me. Inside the skip were a number of bloated, putrefying, semi-clad, distorted bodies; possibly a family ordered into the once empty skip and slain with machine gun fire some days, or weeks, before: it was difficult to tell. This was my first of many encounters with the chilling horror of the Bosnian War. I said nothing to the others, choosing to move back over to the main body of the group, a little numb and slightly perplexed, but continued to eat my lunch. The sight was beyond my ability to react - so I didn't. The rest of the journey was typically uneventful.

We operated from a former Yugoslavian trucking company depot. There were offices, a large workshop, and space to accommodate the thirty or so trucks that the Global Relief Organisation now had in theatre, some of which were bought by the Global Relief Organisation, others donated and in various states of repair.

Every convoy we made required considerable planning and preparation, with the correct amount of rice, wheat, flour, pasta, and medical supplies to be loaded onto each truck. Arrangements would have to be made regarding clearance, enabling us to pass from all military and civil authorities, in the area we would be travelling through.

Not until the most up to date press briefing and security information was available, would the go ahead be given for the warehouse staff to load the trucks for any forthcoming convoy. The mechanics would then make a thorough check of the vehicles - tending to any faults that had been reported. A careful eye was kept on all the trucks; they were not designed for coping with the harsh terrain of mountain passes, and were literally shaken apart, needing constant maintenance.

The locally employed mechanics, drivers, administration assistants and communications specialists, cooks and cleaners provided much needed help. These were relatively well-paid jobs, giving the local economy a boost. All of these workers were committed to their tasks, in particular the vehicle mechanics who worked wonders on the technically advanced trucks that they had not seen before, being used to simple and more rugged Eastern European types.

The Global Relief Organisation quickly organised themselves for the mammoth task of feeding and providing medical assistance to the most needy, from locations all over the Former Yugoslavia.

There were a number of mountain routes that aid convoys used to traverse the Former Yugoslavia. Originating from cart tracks that local villagers had used for centuries, the condition, after numerous heavy vehicles had passed over them, ranged from treacherous, to at best difficult. As the winter of 1993 progressed into 1994, these tracks became nothing more than a sliding, muddy quagmire. However, the British Army were to spend considerable time, manpower and British taxpayers' money, transferring these muddy paths into reasonable quality hard-core type roads, that were to be regularly patrolled by British, French and Spanish United Nations troops.

Route Diamond was the most common route used. Named such by the British Battalion, because, as the name suggests, it was in fact a diamond shaped, one-way clockwise circuit. It covered a hundred or so miles from Split to Livno, a small Bosnian town - and climbed up into the beautiful Raduša Mountains, past the village of Prozor, and onto the British Army Base at Gornji Vakuf.

Occasionally, duties included the immediate evacuation of villages - prior to being overrun by advancing enemy forces. This was preferably done in agreement with the local army commander, be it Serbian, Muslim or Croat. Often, we would have very little time to complete our mission of mercy.

The task of evacuating refugees was sorrowful and distressing. All too frequently, given just an hour to sift through their lifelong possessions, gathering the few belongings we would allow them to take - before their homes were ransacked and burnt to the ground by advancing troops. The 'scorched earth' policy ensured they would never return - having nothing to come back to.

The refugees would be packed like cattle into the back of our trucks. Each were given bottled water and a blanket and driven to relative safety, leaving behind their livestock, pets, and in fact, their whole life. We tried to ensure that families stayed together, but this was difficult, as they were hurriedly herded onto waiting vehicles to an uncertain destiny, all done in close proximity of an active front line. On one occasion, we were forced to travel throughout the night; progress was particularly slow, as the roads near front lines were often strewn with unexploded ordinance and mines that couldn't be seen. Mines were a quick and effective way of prohibiting or slowing the movement of any attacking militia, who were foolish enough to use the roads. Regular infantry would always avoid using roads they hadn't previously made safe. Sometimes we drove around the mines, or had them removed by the local forces that had laid them. Both of these 'mine avoidance' techniques could be very very time consuming, and could result us working for up to twenty hours at a time.

The majority of our trips were to either Zeneca or Tuzla, deep in Bosnia, both besieged city-sized enclaves. The convoy transported much needed food, medicines and as the months passed, cigarettes. Our journeys took us through enchanting woodland and small farming villages, some of which, although deserted, had been spared the physical effects of war. Everywhere we went, it seemed that the local population were suffering from a lack of nicotine as much as the effect of the war itself. Whenever we stopped for a break, or at our final pre-determined destinations, we were constantly asked for cigarettes.

It didn't take long before some of the drivers realised that this was a potential business opportunity. I was earning more money than I had ever earned before, and didn't want to jeopardise a good salary, and would have no part of it. Some drivers, when back in Split, would buy a couple of boxes of two hundred cigarettes from the local market for around seven Deutchemarks, and once successfully in an enclave, sell them for anything between fifty and one hundred Deutchemarks - a very profitable mark up indeed! At one point, a regular supplier who learned of the venture in the Port of Split, approached us with a view of selling the cigarettes directly to us, thus cutting out the market trader and reducing the price to four Deutchemarks per box. In my eyes the extra money really wasn't worth the risk and anyway the Global Relief Organisation and other aid organisations strictly forbade such practice.

If caught by any of the checkpoint guards whilst on convoy, (a distinct possibility as the trucks were often searched) a possible prison sentence, albeit a short one, in some dreary Serbian or Bosnian cell was all that could be realistically looked forward to. I had heard of drivers working for other agencies that had in fact faced such hardship, before being sent home in disgrace, having jeopardised their agencies relief effort for nothing more than a few extra Deutchemarks.

Whilst on convoy we regularly stopped at a village named Ahmići, just outside the small town of Gornji Vakuf. The owner of a local café was in fact a regular cigarette customer. The British had a small garrison nearby, manned, at that time, by the Cheshire Regiment. This gave us a sense of security whilst in the area.

Ahmići was home to about three hundred people. It was a Muslim village and despite the obvious shortages that war brings, life appeared quiet and simple. Any tension, being so near to one of many front lines, didn't seem to show. Grubby children, wearing ill-fitting clothes, played on dirt track roads - chasing convoys of trucks that passed through. Rake thin dogs barked and snapped as they passed by - whilst their parents farmed the land. Livestock grazed in nearby fields. Normality, for now, prevailed in Ahmići.

The middle-aged owner of the local café bar was always pleased to see us, not only did we supply him with the odd box of cigarettes, we proved to be good, regular customers. He in turn sold his surplus cigarettes to his customers and any soldiers passing through. We were probably the best clientele he had, as most of the villagers didn't have much money to spare, living a largely subsistence existence. We always stayed long enough to indulge in Turkish coffee - a black, extremely dreary looking, sugary sludge - guaranteed to rot teeth. Served in small brass cups and tasting awful, it would keep you awake for at least a week. The coffee would be consumed along with petak; a fatty pastry roll filled with something that just about passed as mincemeat. The Former Yugoslavia was some way behind the health conscious West when it came to food. I enjoyed the break, but found the cuisine less than appetising.

En-route to Ahmići, British light tanks would rendezvous with us at a pre-determined point, to escort us through the most dangerous and vulnerable parts of our regular mountain excursions. A tank would lead, with one in the middle and another taking up the rear. This was initially done without the knowledge of the Global Relief Organisation in Belgium. To accept an armed military escort of any description was strictly forbidden (not conducive with the none military image that Global Relief Organisation promoted). I had no qualms about accepting an armed escort and quite enjoyed the experience. Anyway, their lives were not at risk and ours most definitely were: rules and regulations were often conveniently ignored. Military escorts routinely continued: that is until Mark, the Deputy Head of the whole operation arrived from Brussels - to undertake a convoy with us.

Fresh faced Mark was about twenty-five years old and of slight build. He seemed too young for such responsibility and hardly at home in this environment; but who am I to judge. After all, he was committed to helping the needy as much as anyone could be. He chose to travel in my truck, which I wasn't at all happy about. We were all going to have to behave. I for one was not going to be able to upset the other drivers by broadcasting my favourite David Bowie tapes, plus other assortments of eighties music to the rest of the convoy, on the VHF radio. Vince, in turn, was forbidden from broadcasting his selection of distasteful French music. These regular pranks were played to the annoyance of our convoy leader; who regularly lost his temper with us. It was going to be a very boring convoy indeed. Alas, I had no choice.

On arrival at our rendezvous with the tanks, Mark took my radio microphone, and called up the convoy leader, asking for an explanation as to why we were taking an escort. In the same breath, he forbade us from continuing, stating that this was against Global Relief Organisation operational guidelines. To my delight the convoy leader overruled his decision, explaining that he was there as an observer and although he oversaw the Global Relief Organisation operation whilst in Belgium, he had absolutely no authority in the field. Maybe it wasn't going to be such a boring convoy after all! Mark reluctantly accepted this and to my cynical amusement, was soon to learn the dangers of convoy duty, and indeed, why we found it necessary to accept an armed escort.

We approached the safety of the British Army Base at Gornji Vakuf as night was falling. It was forbidden and dangerous to travel at night, as this would attract hostile fire from any nearby-entrenched positions, who would assume they were under attack - shooting first and asking questions later.

Shells were falling nearby; bullets parted the air - making a distinctive zipping sound. The snap as the odd stray round struck my truck made Mark and myself sink low into our seats, as we waited for permission to enter the camp. I could not hide a sly smile as Mark 'the desk' had a taste of what it was really like. He was more used to studying maps and making executive decisions in Brussels, rather than life at the sharp end. A battle was taking place within close proximity of the army camp between Croatian Muslims and non-Muslim Croatians.

We arrived unexpectedly to seek refuge and the British soldiers obligingly moved many of their own vehicles, to accommodate ours.

As we queued outside the camp, in an orderly fashion, each one of our vehicle's registration numbers was taken, along with an inventory of the load. Our personal identification was also thoroughly checked. Meanwhile, the battle around the camp continued. It took some forty-five minutes of stationary vulnerability, before we were finally allowed into the safety of the base. Mark and I remained silent throughout.

Two days later, after returning from this convoy, Mark, in his role as Head of Operations, banned all further convoys that required an armed escort - stating that he did not realise how dangerous the operation had become. He then flew home to continue with his normal job of managing from afar. This gave us a totally welcome, but unexpected break. Two weeks' later, after little aid was delivered, to the now pleading recipients, the Global Relief Organisation, for the first time ever, reluctantly allowed armed escorts into designated areas - thus allowing convoys to resume once more. People were by now beginning to starve to death.

In mid May, whilst returning from Zeneca and travelling at our mandatory full speed, the driver in front of me drove straight into the back of a small, slow moving Bosnian truck, travelling at about 20 mph in the same direction. The convoy speed was approximately 60 mph at the time. It spun around, catapulting the occupants, an elderly couple, through the windscreen and onto the side of the road. The convoy screeched to a halt and I quickly scrambled over to the scene. Upon inspection, the woman seemed to have broken her neck, but miraculously was still alive. The old man's awkwardly configured legs confirmed that they were broken, possibly as he landed, I mused. He was neither breathing nor moving - presumably, the shock of the collision killed him. It was a sorry, pitiful sight, but did not initially cause any of us great concern. On reflection, and no matter how ridiculous it seems to me now, I think my lack of emotion, was due to believing I had to live up to an assumed macho image. I expect the others felt the same.

Local villagers soon arrived and we began to feel a little unsafe, we were unsure of their intentions or if they were going to be hostile. However, they proved to be quite passive and more interested in whether we had any food to give away.

Meanwhile, an ambulance, which was, in fact, a converted estate car, had arrived. The 'ambulance crew', consisting of two scruffy looking youngsters, one of which was wearing an armband displaying the word 'medic', quite simply manhandled the injured woman into the back of the vehicle, showing no respect for her age or injuries. The old man was literally dragged across the road and thrown, unceremoniously, next to her. Shortly afterwards, the villagers, realising we had nothing to give them, returned to their farms and daily life. War had already taken hold of these people and de-sensitised them, for no one, including ourselves, gave more than passing attention to the fate of elderly couple. Neither did anyone appear too concerned about the trauma the surviving old woman would have now been facing as she lay next to her dead husband. Thirteen years on, and on reflection, this was a most inhumane act and completely unforgivable.

After the initial interest and excitement of the accident had passed, my thoughts became focused on what time we were likely to get back to Split, after this unexpected delay. What shall I have to eat? Would I have time for a shower before going out? I was also becoming de-sensitised as I viewed the terrible suffering of this couple as nothing more than an inconvenience to my social schedule.

We continued our journey and arrived on the outskirts of Gornji Vakuf, some two miles away from the British UN Army Base. The local militia decided not to allow us to pass the checkpoint, nor could we afford another delay, as we wouldn't make it back by nightfall. The British soldiers at the UN base, who were monitoring our radio transmissions, sent down two light Scimitar tanks to escort us through - with approximately twenty soldiers. The militia was having none of it and made a show of cocking their weapons; a very aggressive gesture indeed. At this point, having ventured out of my truck to see what was going on, I decided to make a quick exit, walking back to my truck. A militiaman pointed his AK47 machine gun in my direction. I froze on the spot; my boss told me to go to my truck, but my boss did not have a gun, so I stayed where I was; only moving away when the militia man's attention was diverted elsewhere. A 'stand off' soon materialised between the poorly armed - but hardened militia - and the well-armed, disciplined soldiers of the British Army.

After some negotiation between the British Army Commanding Officer and the Militia Commander, the British tanks withdrew and we returned to our lorries. It became apparent, twelve hours later, that locally organised militia supporting the Croatian cause had stopped us from proceeding. They were unwilling to let us pass, as two of their own soldiers had been kidnapped by Bosnian Muslim forces. It was nothing to do with us, but they wanted the British to put pressure on the Muslim Commander for their release.

The British Army thoroughly looked after us, bringing freshly made sandwiches and drinks. The four Scimitar light tanks and supporting soldiers remained with us for protection. I wonder what Mark, in his office in Brussels, would have made of that! I felt quite proud that the British forces took our safety so seriously. These young men, some of whom I had the opportunity to talk to, were itching for a fight and seemed very disappointed when none materialised; I was not. They seemed keen to avenge the death of one of their colleagues, Private Karl Briggs, himself a Scimitar tank driver who was recently shot through his head by a sniper, whilst driving his tank through Gornji Vakuf. His armoured vehicle veered off the road into the river, slightly injuring the other crewmembers. No one really knew which side had shot him, but to these soldiers, the killing of any Bosnian, Croat, or Serb would do. A memorial stone erected by his company marked the spot of his death. Villagers, disappointed by the UN mission, later desecrated this.

We spent the afternoon drinking with the militia that held us. They had, by now mellowed considerably, confessing that they were very sorry for stopping us from proceeding, and that they had in fact the utmost respect for the Global Relief Organisation - and the neutral status of all aid organisations. Their commander reminded us that they were only following orders. As long as no one was hurt, that was fine by me.

The British Commander did apply some pressure for the release of the Croatians and their corpses were duly returned. The bodies were delivered in an old hastily camouflaged green and black Ford pick up truck. I was fascinated by the German World War II machine gun mounted on the back, with a shiny belt of ammunition trailing from its breach. The delivery of the bodies was a very ordered and calm event. The pick up driver got out of his seat, went to the back of the pick up, dropped the tailgate and the militia did the rest. The dead soldiers' hands had been tied behind their backs, and killed with a single shot to the back of their heads. At least that part of their ordeal would have been painless. Ultimately, as agreed with the Militia Commander, we were allowed to proceed on our return journey to Split. As we had some way to go and it was getting dark, we hurried into the confines of the British Base at Gornji Vakuf.

At that time, the Croats and Muslims were fighting with desperation for control of Gornji Vakuf. The Croats were determined to evict the Muslims and vice-versa. Unfortunately, the British base was located directly between the opposing forces.

As darkness began to fall, the surrounding gunfire became more intense and we were ordered into shelter. The majority of us, whom incidentally chose to sit outside on some empty ammunition boxes, in order to watch the most amazing 'fireworks display', foolishly ignored the instruction to keep undercover. None of us realised how dangerous it was.

Tracer rounds sped across the sky overhead, seeking out targets hidden in buildings - mortars erupted amongst the rubble and stray rounds entered the camp. It was noisy and frightening but also very exciting. An ammunition dump, the size of a small village, blew up only two miles away; for some fleeting moments turning night into day - sending rockets into the air. This, coupled with the noise of an incalculable amount of other detonating ordinance, was a truly deafening and absolutely spectacular sight. A mortar smashed through the roof of the toilet block in the camp, completely demolishing it. One disgruntled soldier, who had recently vacated the toilet, casually commented how he hoped it would be re-built in the morning, as he had the 'runs'.

In the days and nights that followed, British soldiers would, in turn, occupy sandbag emplacements, on top of the roof of the main accommodation building in the camp. They would scan the surrounding area with their rifle mounted night sights, searching out any Croatians or Bosnian Muslims, that were taking it upon themselves to fire into the camp. They seemed happy to undertake the duty that they had spent so much time training and preparing for. In fact, they were most gratified at having successfully engaged, and probably killing soldiers, of a largely untrained but potentially merciless 'enemy'.

A couple of days later, the unenviable position of being stuck between two opposing forces, intent on killing each other began to have an effect upon me. Stray rounds frequently hit the buildings and vehicles around us, but fortunately, no one to my knowledge, had been hit in the camp. I was becoming somewhat agitated at the helplessness felt by having to endure constant incoming small arms fire, whilst trapped in the base where I had made new friends. I was telling one of them that I had never fired one of the new SA80 rifles that the British Army was now using, having been trained, and becoming a marksman on the SA80s predecessor, the 7.62mm Self Loading Rifle (SLR). The Belgian designed SLR was a more accurate, reliable and considerably more powerful weapon than the lighter - historically troublesome, British designed SA80. The SLR was originally commissioned for British Army use when they still had the remnants of an empire to police. Power and range were more important than falling into place with the NATO led Americans who used the smaller, far less lethal 5.56mm round that the SA80 also used. The logic being that for every man injured and not killed by the smaller round, took two other men to look after him. As a soldier, I would have sooner gone to the recent Gulf War with an SLR and its built in reliability and range, rather than this new weapon. I explained to my new friend how I would like to have the opportunity to fire an SA80. He took my 'not so subtle hint' and after giving me a quick run down of the weapon, we slipped stealthily away, finding a sheltered secluded spot in the vehicle park.

After clearly identifying muzzle flashes some two hundred yards away, with my pulse pounding in my head, we took up a position overlooking the direction of the incoming fire. We had found an excellent vantage point, providing reasonable cover, and a good overview of the 'target area'. The soldier I was with drew a pistol that he was carrying. Not wanting to harm anyone, but nevertheless keen to try out this new weapon, I had the satisfaction of firing into an empty gun position near to the 'hostile' positions. It must have been scary for any Bosnian or Croatian soldiers in nearby emplacements but I didn't care. As I had previously been trained; aiming and firing between breaths, holding the weapon snugly into my shoulder and resting the stock in my left hand, with a firmer hold of the pistol grip with my right; I calmly emptied the whole of the thirty-round magazine, in controlled three round bursts. This pretty much demolished the crates and sandbags that made up the position.

'That was fuckin' great!' I said bashfully to the accompanying soldier, knowing that I had done nothing more than shoot up a wall of sandbags. He smiled as I gave the rifle back to him and we quickly exited the area, just in case of any return fire. There wasn't any. The firing of the SA80 certainly felt good at the time and was a definite release of the ongoing tension that I was feeling.

The next day word soon got around of my exploit the night before. I sheepishly played down the whole occurrence and told everyone that the whole idea of me firing a weapon in the middle of a firefight was totally absurd. If the Global Relief Organisation in Belgium had found out, I would have been in trouble and no doubt sent home, having clearly breached the Global Relief Organisation strict rules.

Three days later, having thoroughly outstayed our welcome, largely due to my German colleagues taking over the satellite TV, (much to the distress of the British soldiers and myself), we continued our journey back to the safety of Split, Croatia. Driving through destroyed Gornji Vakuf, whilst firefights continued, proved to be quite harrowing. Neither side had gained an advantage and were engaged in house to house fighting. I was most afraid as I left the safety of the British Base and had the impression that I was not the only one trying to hide my fear. It took both considerable effort and concentration to try to stop my legs from shaking and from speaking in a slightly higher octave than normal. This, being the first of many occasions when I tried unsuccessfully not to do either.

Like the rest of us, I had little option but to go along with the situation, choosing not to think too much about it, but nonetheless scared stiff at the absurdity of having to drive through what was essentially an active battlefield, with the warring parties engaged in fierce house-to-house combat. How I hid my fear as well as I did, I shall never know. On the other hand, perhaps I didn't.

I was in a heightened state of alert as we moved off in convoy, adrenaline pumped vigorously through my veins. My breathing intensified and my senses felt as though they were about to explode. I hoped that the blue and white Global Relief Organisation flags that we had all erected on our trucks would be respected - at least on this occasion - if no other. If it was not, I would be dead in the next few minutes - it was that simple - and I knew it. As we exited the camp, I felt my legs begin to shake even more - at the same time wondering if anyone else have the same problem - I hoped so. We drove up the rough track towards the main road that took us right into the centre of Gornji Vakuf where the fighting was most intensive. This was lunacy, I said aloud to myself, hoping at least God would hear me and temporarily put a stop to the fighting. As I approached the main road, I could hear the sound of machine gunfire getting louder. Mortars exploded and the whoosh and detonation of RPGs (Rocket Propelled Grenades) impacted all around me. My God, are we really going to drive through this? My panic-stricken face must have said it all. One of us, if not all of us were going to die. Even if no one shot directly at us, there was surely too many stray rounds flying around for us to make it safely.

    I actually think that the fighting forces were so amazed at us driving through the mayhem, or were so astonished at what was such a foolhardy (or brave) act that, by the time they realised what was happening, we were all but through the killing zone. On the other hand, maybe the white and blue of Global Relief Organisation was respected after all. I was so afraid that after the first three hundred yards I began to focus on nothing more than the road in front of me. My innocence preventing me from looking around for fear of what I might see. This was not a wise or sensible thing to do as I was severely limiting my 'situational awareness', thus restricting my ability to react to immediate danger; even if it was only to duck my head behind the steering wheel. I guess I was basically just burying my head in the sand, as my senses tried to absorb my fear and the atrocious scene.

    Despite some near misses, with a bewildered looking Croatian soldier pointing his AK47 assault machine gun directly at me, and firing above my truck (at which point I believed in all sincerity that I was about to be shot), the convoy passed through relatively unscathed. Some of the trucks had superficial damage caused by shrapnel or the odd bullet but nothing serious. I began to breathe more normally and unwind a little as the noise and danger receded into the background. When my pulse had returned to something like normal, I began to think about the experience and vowed, in future, to always remain aware of everything that was happening around me, and not become transfixed like a startled rabbit caught in the headlamps of a car - when driving through danger.

There were many dead lining the streets we had just driven through, some with their arms and legs in bloody, pulverised khaki or camouflaged tatters, others barely recognisable as human beings - resembling a butcher's pile of offal. A number of the recognisable dead or badly wounded were already booby-trapped with anti-personnel mines. If anyone, such as a wife of the dead soldier, or member of the family tried to move them, they would also be maimed or killed. The mines were placed underneath the dying, or dead victim, catching out any unsuspecting person who was not privy to this particularly cruel aspect of war.

Abandoned broken weapons lay in the road alongside the dead and wounded. My God, is this war in reality? I should have known by now, but seeing really *is* believing. This was as real as it gets, and I was noticeably shaken - we all were.

Twenty minutes later, we arrived back at Ahmići, looking forward to a much-needed relaxing break to talk the normal drivel that men talk when they are scared shitless - and trying not to show it - after the harrowing experience of Gornji Vakuf.

The road sign indicating our arrival lay twisted on the road. The mosque in Ahmići was on fire, its spire having crashed to the ground. All other buildings, houses, shops, farm outhouses were nothing more than smouldering ruins. A village, a people, a heritage destroyed.

An acrid smell of death hung in the motionless silent air. Vehicles littered the roads. People who had tried to escape with their families now lay dead and bloody inside their small trucks and Zastava cars, each riddled with bullet holes or ripped open by exploding shells. Some slumped forward; their heads pressed hard against cracked windscreens after veering off the road, crashing into buildings and trees. Dead mothers held lifeless children in their arms, in a vein attempt to protect them with their own bodies as shrapnel sliced them apart. Others lay lifeless nearby; killed after trying to escape from their immobilised cars and burning buildings: caught whilst running and exposed to withering Croat fire - trying to evade the creeping Croatian artillery and subsequent ground forces. The few personal belongings they carried scattered around them...

Tractor and truck engines gently idled away against a silent, motionless, eerie background - obediently waiting to move their now dead cargo. Livestock lay dead in the surrounding fields, slaughtered along with the population in the frantic unrelenting killing frenzy. Occasionally, a tethered dog would bark, calling for a master who would never return...

Our coffee shop was also a smouldering mess, the owner nowhere to be seen. On the road outside was a coach that was tightly packed with black, charred, grotesquely, twisted bodies, some with a skeletal grin staring skywards, most of their flesh having been burned away. Other corpses lay faced down. Many had limbs turned in on themselves in what seemed like the only way to cope with the extreme pain of being burned alive. Evidently, the victims had been herded onto the coach and set alight. The men and women tending their fields, children who had been playing in the streets - burned alive.

I felt removed from reality, as though the scene was played out through the windscreen of my truck, in slow motion, somehow separating me from the scene I now witnessed. United Nations investigators later found the remains of a three-year-old child, who had been doused in petrol and set alight. I was pleased that I didn't see this for myself... I had seen enough already. All this took place within three miles of a British Army Base.

There was no chatter on the short-range VHF radios in the trucks. Everyone was silently stunned, absorbing the memorable sight and personally coming to terms with the atrocity that had taken place. Ahmići simply did not any exist. The entire village and population of three hundred annihilated. I covered my face with my hands and cried in an effort to rid myself of the anger, and complete sense of helplessness and bitterness, that I was now feeling. With each tear, I lost some of the innocence and faith in human kind, that until now, I had managed to retain: this didn't stop the overwhelming sense of grief I was feeling. What could I do? I was later to learn that the nearby British soldiers at Vitez army base shared my sense of anguish. They were ordered, reluctantly, to stand by as the killing took place. At that time, and throughout the war, they had a completely ineffective United Nations Mandate, which would not allow them to interfere. I later heard that one soldier was so distressed by the atrocious scenes that he attempted to commit suicide. Such was the sight of the massacre.

We resumed our journey in silence, leaving the carnage behind us. Some of us forever changed: all of us a lot less naive to the consequence of war.

We still had to get back to Split before nightfall and whilst travelling through the nearby ruins of Vitez, adjacent to the British Base, an explosion occurred some fifteen feet to the left of my vehicle, showering it with debris. My thoughts were still very much with the dead people of Ahmići. I was again driving in a trance-like state, despite only hours before, vowing not to allow myself to become so distanced from reality.

The small but loud explosion quickly brought me back to reality. There was some prattle on the radios but after Ahmići, one small explosion didn't really excite us. I believe someone had either thrown a grenade, or a small mortar had been aimed at the convoy. This turned out to be the first of several times I faced direct hostility.

As I drove, my mind started to drift again and I began to think about the small detonation. Had someone tried to kill me? Why for God's sake? Was it personal? Did they not realise the Global Relief Organisation was not on anybody's side. My spirits dropped even further as I suddenly became aware that I too might end up another faceless or scarred casualty of this war.

Once back at our warehouse and in comfortable and familiar surroundings, discussion about Ahmići and the grenade attack on the convoy quickly subsided. In fact, it soon ceased to enter conversation at all; strangely, as convoy drivers, we felt bizarrely proud at having been bloodied. Gung-ho bravado prevailed.

After taking the mini-bus back to my apartment in Split and alone, I was no longer obliged to display a bold 'no fear' image and could just be the frightened human being that I really was. I sat on my bed in complete silence contemplating and coming to terms with just how easy it is to be killed here in Bosnia. I hoped the other drivers were feeling the same. It was not just an exciting adventure. My job took on a completely new meaning and now became an experience that I, as an individual, had to come to terms with. For the first time since my arrival, I started to put up defensive barriers and viewed the victims of this war not as real people, but inanimate objects awaiting a premature death. On reflection I realise this was nothing more than self-preservation and to some extent a selfish coping mechanism, which I would choose to use whenever it suited me. The easiest way for me to cope was by not openly caring or feeling any grief. Nevertheless, I did go on to modify my personal coping strategy, as I was to be in an environment where prolific killing was almost a daily occurrence, ultimately penetrating all my emotional defences and making it *my* war.

Despite witnessing the drama and horrors unfold at Ahmići, Gornji Vakuf and Vitez, most convoys were happily to prove quite uneventful. The countryside was beautiful and yet an extremely dangerous, totally lawless part of the world to be in at this time. Occasionally, refugees were evacuated or food distributed as shelling and firefights took place around us. It was at times frightening and nearly always unpredictable, but the camaraderie, completely unparalleled in normal life, somehow made the experience worthwhile. I miss that camaraderie to this day and don't expect to have the opportunity to repeat it. My colleagues were my family and we were all very close.

We continued making our regular trips to Zeneca, delivering food and medicines, staying in a most appalling hotel. It was war and the staff did their best, but rancid goat's cheese and stale bread wasn't the best way to start the day. We ate it and accepted that an upset stomach and constant diarrhoea were just another consequence of war.

When in Zeneca, I would often meet up with friends from other organisations and spend time catching up chatting about home etc. We would meet outside the hotel reception where a number of young girls, who appeared to be about sixteen years old, would gather. They would then follow us to a local 'burger bar' - burgers happily consumed but no doubt made from the few remaining dogs in the city (I became very ill shortly after). The girls would wait outside, and then follow us back to our hotels. It soon became evident that they were quite willing to prostitute themselves. A small number of my friends took advantage of this, paying the equivalent of $2.50 for full sex. This disturbed and shocked me somewhat, but I never spoke out against it, despite the moral objections that might be raised.

On one occasion, I walked into a room without knocking and found two of my recently made friends with a young girl, all three completely naked and seemingly enjoying the experience. They found it mildly amusing that they only gave her ten Deutchemarks - between them. I guess this only served to remind me that there are no rules in war and that morality takes a distant second place to survival. The regular visits by the 'prostitutes' continued throughout the summer.

Chapter Two

As the war progressed, both civilians and military endured new horrors and starvation. Food became scarce and clean water almost unobtainable.

September 10th, 1993 - a date remembered with revulsion. The scenes I was about to witness were reminiscent of silent black and white newsreels and photographic images of World War II concentration camps... As if Nuremberg had never happened.

At 4.00 am, a typical bright, refreshing autumn morning, a convoy of six trucks departed for a 'holding centre' in Southern Croatia. It was a makeshift Croatian camp, not a prisoner of war camp, temporarily housing soldiers captured in recent fighting. Hastily gathered, prior to being despatched to an official prisoner of war camp, where they would come under the protection of the Red Cross. Under international law, only the Red Cross can work in prisoner of war camps. We would never have been allowed to enter. The improvised camp housed both Bosnian Muslim and Croatian men, some of whom had previously fought side by side with their captors against the Serbs, but now due to political encumbrance, were at war with each other. The holding centre guards were expecting us and quickly swung open the black wrought iron gates.

Our trucks were loaded with blankets, soap, detergent, toiletries, clothing, and a large amount of tinned food, mainly corned beef, and vegetables, along with sacks of beans. All of which was unloaded into a makeshift store by the captured soldiers. The majority of the goods were purchased in Croatia or given to us by other organisations keen to see their supplies put to good use. As an independent outfit, we were often asked to help other small organisations that hadn't much in the way of transport.

After initial discussion and exchange of formalities with the guards, we parked our trucks up as directed. The detainees that were still healthy formed queues from the trucks to the storeroom. One by one, the bags of flour and boxes of food were passed down the queue to be locked safely away.

Toiletries were issued personally to the prisoners, but I doubt whether they saw much of the food. The guards all looked very well fed. Medical supplies, intended for sick and wounded captives could quite conceivably have ended up in the nearest Croatian Army Field Hospital, despite the checks the Global Refugee Organisation made. It was an unfortunate and unavoidable fact that an estimated 25% of all donations ended up supporting the war effort for one side or another. However, I believe this eventuality was far out weighed by the lives saved through the nationwide assistance provided.

The rough and ready site held approximately four hundred men of various ages, who were mainly conscripted soldiers. Two hundred or so were housed in two large hanger-type buildings, so tightly packed that there wasn't enough room for them to lie down - not that they had mattresses or blankets to lie on anyway. Sanitation consisted of an exposed gutter at one end of the hanger. There was very little ventilation and in the late summer heat, the stench from so many unwashed bodies was completely overwhelming. Others were kept in a nearby cave. Inmates were confined within the hanger, or cave, for approximately twenty-three and a half hours per day. For those in the cave, in complete darkness, with nothing more than the odd bucket for sanitation. The conditions were even more appalling than those in the hangar. The air was suspended with bad breath, smoke and the sweaty odour of crowded grimy men: rancid condensation trickled down the walls.

The camp had once been one of the many now deserted factories that kept the local population in employment prior to the war. The cave was once an old storage facility. The gates and surrounding fencing were hastily, but liberally interwoven with layers of menacing razor-edged barbed wire, between what was left of the old iron fence.

Some of the captured soldiers were fortunate enough to have jobs around the camp - cooking and cleaning. Of these many wandered around aimlessly, not sure of whom they were, or what they were doing. Their uniforms were already starting to rot away. Others were naked and in a complete daze, urinating and defecating where they stood - still recovering from the shock of recent battles. Their emaciated bodies were often unable to carry out the simple tasks they were given - quickly becoming breathless and weak and succumbing to the inhumane conditions of incarceration. The guards taunted them and seemed amused by the lack of response they received from such individuals. All but the most recently detained were suffering from the effects of malnourishment. Others were already well on their way to death.

Those not fortunate enough to have the freedom to work around the camp had between ten and fifteen minutes of liberty, twice daily, whilst queuing up for a chunk of bread and half a bowl of watered down broth. There were five bowls, five mugs, and five spoons - for all six hundred inmates! A queue of fifty would form, standing in a rigid line. The first ten to be fed would get permission to leave the queue and run as best they could to the soup cauldron, where they would be given their gruel - overlooked by intimidating armed guards. The prisoners stooped to the ground, hastily pouring soup down their gullets, some of which spilled down their already filthy clothing, at the same time tearing at the chunk of bread, having only seconds to consume the food, before running back to the next man in the queue. They passed on the unwashed utensils, encouraging the spread of hepatitis and typhoid, then dragged themselves back into the cave or hanger, for a further prolonged spell of dungeon like incarceration. The feeding process continued throughout the day.

The captured men seemed very frightened of the guards, but this didn't stop them from taking off their shirts, almost in unison, to show us their skeletal bodies. The only weapon they had to further their cause. It was generally understood that a number of prisoners had been executed. Some, I was told, were ordered to dig their own graves, then lie in them and say their prayers - before being shot. Others were never to have the luxury of a grave and were left to rot in the fields and woods that they were cut down in. This was backed up by a number of captives who risked their lives, or at least being severely beaten, by talking to me. One in particular, spoke very good English and told of daily executions taking place in, and outside the camp, whilst on 'work' parties.

Against my principles, I gave the English-speaking prisoner one of the army ration packs that I carried in case of emergency. He tore open the foil lid and scooped up the pasta and meat with his bare filthy hands, such was his hunger.

'Tell the world, tell the world what is happening here, please please help us!' he would say between gulping down mouthfuls of food - as I looked on completely bemused and unsure of how to react.

Allegedly, when fresh prisoners arrived and were yet to be interrogated, guards would open the doors of either the hanger or the cave and fire their machine guns, killing a number of inmates and making room for the newly captured ones. This would be done in full view of the newly arrived, leaving them in no doubt about the kind of regime they were entering. It would also encourage them to 'talk' during subsequent questioning.

Evidence of this slaughter was apparent by bullet holes in the walls at a place indicated by one of the prisoners, who was also a fluent English speaker. I have little reason to doubt, judging by the conditions, that what I was told was true.

The camp hospital was a garden shed, approximately ten feet by ten. Beds were stacked three high, with two or three prisoners to a bed, whilst others were on the floor. The patients, all young soldiers previously shot or suffering other wounds, were pale and hollow eyed, some looked close to death. Upon entering, merely to look around, the more conscious prisoners reached out and began to plead with me in their native language. Their blood-soaked bandaged, torn bodies struggled to survive in appalling, stiflingly hot, cramped inhumane conditions. The 'doctor' appeared genuinely ashamed. He also pleaded for help asking for more equipment. Another English-speaking inmate beckoned me over to his bed. He told me that the 'hopeless cases' were taken outside and shot to make bed space for new arrivals. He explained that the doctor had no real control over the fate of the patients and was unable to prevent this.

I was later to speak of the camp and what I had witnessed on BBC Radio, remembering what had been asked of me. In truth, the West, after viewing news coverage of such camps, already knew of their existence, but perhaps did not want to acknowledge what was happening there. Throughout my visit, a Reuters Press team filmed the camp and tried to interview me. I offered no comment.

As the afternoon wore on, the guards sensed our displeasure at the conditions and began to act in a particularly pleasant and courteous manner to the prisoners. They offered cigarettes to them, whilst saying,

'We are friends.' The prisoners seemed startled by this unusual behaviour and hesitated in accepting the offering, unsure of how to react.

The Camp Commander offered the Global Relief Organisation staff lunch in his quarters. Beef and vegetables were on offer. As a mark of respect to the prisoners, my boss declined the offer of lunch. We left for the pleasant coastal road to Split in the late afternoon.

A few days later, after negotiation with the Croat authorities we returned to the Camp with a convoy of buses. It seemed that a number of the inmates were not going to a prisoner of war camp after all. The mission was to evacuate the worst two hundred or so of the most emaciated and sick prisoners, to a small island off the coast of Croatia, whereupon they would become refugees under the protection of the United Nations, and housed in what were formerly tourist hotels.

The list of names was read out to the prisoners selected for evacuation as they stood quietly in the hot sun - on parade. They were then herded onto the coaches by the waiting guards. Some fainted and others protested, bravely saying that they would not go if their comrades and relatives could not go with them. They were not at liberty to make that decision. However, the gesture did not go unnoticed by either the Global Relief Organisation staff or the guards. Their comrades pushed them forward ensuring they take advantage of this one-off life saving offer.

Once on the coach each was given a bottle of fresh water and a small bar of chocolate and nothing more. To give them too much after being on a starvation diet could make them very ill, or quite easily kill them. It would take time for their bodies to adjust to a normal balanced diet - requiring specialist intervention to help get them back to their normal body weight.

Whilst the prisoners were boarding the buses, local villagers started to gather outside the camp gates. The guards were seemingly indifferent but refused to let us out, stating that it would be dangerous. This turned out to be true and after a couple of hours, I began to realise that the local populace were opposed to the prisoner release. The local Croats, wanted their men folk (who had been captured by the Bosnians) released, in return for the freedom being offered to the Bosnian Muslims. This was an entirely reasonable request. They weren't to know that negotiations were taking place between the Bosnian and Croatian governments who, despite the state of war, and with the help of another non-government organisation, managed to keep dialogue open. The local villagers, who were being addressed through the camp perimeter wire by a Global Relief Organisation official, simply did not believe him.

The situation slowly began to deteriorate. Our vehicles that were parked outside the camp were smashed up by this angry mob that, by now, numbered some three hundred people.

After around nine hours, with the detainees sitting patiently on the oven-like coaches in the stifling sun, the Camp Commander ordered his guards to force open the gates. Our small convoy began pushing its way through the mass of angry people. I was on the lead coach: the driver was struggling not to run down any of our assailants. Without warning, house bricks and stones shattered the windows, striking some of the released detainees; two teenage lads, about nineteen years of age, sitting on the front seat, sat terrified hugging each other. They knew that if this 'lynch mob' boarded, they, along with myself, would have been savagely beaten and possibly killed in a frenzy of violence. The coach, driven by locally employed drivers from Split, came to a halt after only a few feet from the camp gates. The mob swarmed around it and began to rock it violently, seemingly trying to overturn it. The driver froze terrified at the wheel. One hysterical youth tried to gain entry by forcing the sliding doors open. I was scared and reacted by hanging from the grab rail above me, and kicking him swiftly, and as hard as I could in his face. He fell back helplessly into the crowd, with his nose obviously broken and mouth bloodied. 'Bastard' I thought. Unsurprisingly, the sight of the bloodied youth enraged the crowd further. The jeering, along with determined volleys of bricks and stones increased. Some of the women in the crowd were screaming - shouting was now at fever pitch. Most of the windows on the coaches had by now been smashed; occupants huddled on the floor, cowering between seats. I was both excited and afraid but knew I had to control my fear. The situation was getting out of control so, above the sound of smashing glass, I shouted and gestured at the driver to force his way through - as I crouched behind his seat taking cover.

'Run the fuckers over if you have to!' I bellowed in English at the top of my voice. I think he understood me. Without much encouragement and no doubt as frightened as I was, he regained his composure, and forced his way through without running anyone over. Pistol shots were fired from the crowd,

'IDEMO! IDEMO! IDEMO!' ('GO! GO! GO!') I shouted.

Once clear of the crowd the released men began to return to their seats, nurse each other, and relax a little, whilst talking quietly amongst themselves. They were happy to be alive and so was I. I made my way to the back of the coach to distribute more water. Many grabbed my hand and repeatedly thanked me, making gestures, which indicated they were pleased with how I dealt with the youth who tried to board the coach. I wasn't so happy, knowing how ugly it could have become. The whole situation was barely under control.

As the journey continued the coach load of released men were soon to suffer further indignities at the hands of armed Croatian police, who insisted on them disembarking at every checkpoint we came to. They said they were searching for weapons. None were found. We arrived at our destination at 2.30 am the following day.

I was very tired and glad it was all over. The incident at the camp could have been a lot worse but fortunately wasn't, so there was no point giving it any more thought. I had not slept for over twenty-four hours and still had to get back to Split after only a cursory couple of hours sleep in a truck.

The prisoners were to be well looked after on the island with beds to sleep in, regular meals, and quality medical attention. They were the lucky ones. A good many that were transferred to prisoner of war camps did not survive the war, dying in indignant squalor.

Chapter Three

Virtually no food, medicine, or water, left the population impoverished: ammunition was in short supply. The collapse of the Muslim sector seemed imminent, leaving the women in fear of being enslaved and raped and the male population in fear of being executed.

November 1993 saw Mostar, the capital of the Herzegovina region of Bosnia in a desperate situation. The River Neretva, served as a front line between the conflicting sides. One side of the river was predominantly Bosnian Croat, the other Bosnian Muslim. Both were fighting for control of this beautiful ancient city, built in the Ottoman Empire by the Turks. The architecture was typical of the time with buildings constructed of hand-carved stone and, until the war, largely unspoilt. The city had until fairly recent times been an idyllic escape for many European tourists. Sadly, vast areas had now been reduced to rubble and the famous arched stone bridge, built in 1566; linking the two ethnically divided sides had been totally destroyed, making the division of the two communities symbolically complete.

Our convoy made its way with some trepidation deep into the suburbs of Mostar. We remained constantly aware of the threat from snipers located on the other side of the river. Explosions and gunfire were in abundance. The Bosnian Muslim soldiers at the last checkpoint, before entering the town, advised us not to proceed even though we were taking aid to their own people. They said it was just too dangerous and seemed genuinely concerned for our safety. Although grateful for their advice, I had mentally prepared myself for getting right into the thick of an ongoing battle and didn't want to turn around with a full consignment of aid. I was also just a little bit excited at going deep into the heart of the city. Nevertheless, we should have heeded their advice. The convoy leader briefly discussed the situation with us, we decided to proceed after having come this far. Earlier that day we came under mortar fire at a particularly dangerous stretch of road. I think this had psychologically prepared us for more to come. No one was hit, but there was no point in running the gauntlet on the way back with a full load - all for nothing. This was the only chance of aid the half-starved people in Mostar would have for some time. Many people were already weak from hunger and the more vulnerable were beginning to die, succumbing to illness brought about by poor sanitation and malnourishment. Both the Serbs and Croats had blockaded the predominantly Muslim part of the city; they had not received supplies for seven weeks. Starvation was a primitive but effective weapon of war and one readily employed by all sides whenever possible.

As we drove down the streets people started to appear at windows and doors, after emerging from their damp candle lit cellars. Many, though looking gaunt and pale, started to cheer and clap as we drove down the streets towards our unloading point. I didn't pay much attention to them but felt quite proud. We hadn't come to liberate them and free them from the horror of war - but merely to bring in desperately needed supplies: supplies, that in my opinion, may only serve to put off an inevitable end. Anyway, I was too busy looking for sniper vantage points and boltholes just in case I came under fire to be bothered by the 'welcoming' onlookers. Our progress was slow as we had many obstacles to negotiate: burnt out cars and fallen walls all had to carefully driven over or bulldozed through. This gave the younger people in Mostar, the opportunity to run from cover and mob the slowly moving trucks, pulling at the tarpaulin sheets covering the load and stealing as many small bags of flour as they could before falling off in to the road - bags bursting on the ground around them as they fled the scene. Others ran forward to scoop up as much of the spilt flour as they could - such was their desperation.

Each one of the five trucks unloaded into a former shop in the main street. A number of local Global Relief Organisation volunteers came to help. Every truck was carrying approximately ten tons of flour or rice as well as important medical equipment.

One vehicle at a time moved forward to be unloaded, whilst the others stayed hidden between buildings further down the street, so as not to present too much of a lucrative and easy target, for Croatian artillery spotters, hidden in the surrounding vicinity.

Unloading was done by hand, as the war continued around us unabated. The sides of the vehicles were stripped down and a human chain hastily formed. Young and old emerged from their broken homes and began helping pass the provisions into the relative safety of the stone buildings. Shells and mortars were incoming but I was too busy to be scared. Bullets and shrapnel hit the walls above us and ricocheted around us, tearing into the tarpaulin covers on the trucks and striking the cabs. This in itself was not terribly unnerving, since I was by now becoming somewhat accustomed to war and largely able to keep under cover. Plenty of local young volunteers seemed keen to expose themselves to the possibility of an early death. We'd done our bit, I thought. The rest is up to them.

Despite the obvious precaution of not exposing ourselves to hostile fire any longer than we had to, Hervé, the thirty year old French convoy leader and myself had very lucky escapes. Hervé, standing in the shop doorway, barely escaped death from a bullet that struck the wall behind him - only six inches above his head. At the time, I was in an adjoining room and decided to take a quick look through the window to see how the locals were doing. As I momentarily marvelled at the speed at which the locals were unloading the trucks, two bullets shattered the window near to where I stood. The first one struck the windowpane and wall behind me, before coming to rest on the floor. The second also hit the wall, ricocheted haphazardly around the room before finally settling on the floor. By extreme luck, both having missed me. The experience is really nothing like in the movies, with people ducking and diving when under fire, it all happens very quickly and you are either alive or dead

- it's that simple. I expect that all three bullets were some of the many hundreds of strays flying indiscriminately around the city as the orgy of killing continued - around the clock.

Meanwhile, soldiers were returning from the front line, a number of British Mercenaries included, handing their weapons to other young men due to go to the front. Throughout the war, there was always a shortage of weapons in the Bosnian sector of Mostar. Many of these boys would not see the next day, going to their duty with only thirty or so rounds of ammunition, but nevertheless keeping the Croatian forces guessing at their real strength and consequently keeping them at bay. I am sure that if the better-equipped Croats knew just how short of ammunition the Bosnian Muslims were, they would have launched an offensive and simply swept through the city.

I later learned that the Croat Commander, (who was at war with both the Bosnian Serbs and the Bosnian Muslims) would telephone the Bosnian Serbs to request, and often receive, artillery support, striking Muslim positions from Serbian guns located in the nearby hills. This was incredibly confusing and quite bizarre, as they would often exchange artillery fire themselves; such was the incredulity and confusion of the Bosnian War.

After my truck was unloaded, I reversed away from the shop and stayed in my cab. A group had gathered and begun to beg for food. It was quite frustrating, as I had nothing to give except my own food that I carried in case I ever became stranded. A woman in her early fifties stood nearby; she occasionally looked at me but said nothing. By now the group, realising that I wasn't going to give them anything, had diverted their attention to the other drivers. I beckoned her over and again against my principles, gave her one of my two emergency ration packs. She nodded her head in acknowledgement and walked away. Some minutes later, she returned with a full bottle of Cognac and passed it to me discretely. I didn't drink, but accepted her gift anyway, believing that it would be discourteous not to. If not for my consumption, I was sure it could be bartered for something useful for me sometime.

Soon after, what turned out to be her daughter appeared. She was about twenty years old, slim and attractive with long, shiny healthy looking black hair. Her name was Maria. She spoke a little English.

Immediately attracted to her I locked my truck up and sat with her on a nearby doorstep, communicating in a combination of English, French and Bosnian. The war raged on around us. There were still a number of trucks to be unloaded and I knew we wouldn't be leaving Mostar for at least two more hours. Despite not knowing her, I locked my now empty truck up and followed her to her home, where her family greeted me. I didn't even tell anyone where I was going, which was somewhat foolish. My trust had been bought with a bottle of cognac, but I somehow trusted her; perhaps it was her gentle trusting smile and beautiful big brown eyes, or most probably my desire to spend time with an attractive woman in the midst of war. The opportunity having arisen, I instantly felt that I needed to be with her.

Her house was one of the very few not damaged by shellfire. I was offered homemade cake but politely refused; I did not want to take any of their valuable food away from them.

Maria, like the rest of the people in Mostar was distraught and kept thanking me for coming to help her people. She decided she would like to show me what was left of the town she lived in. I agreed. I usually only ever drove through the destruction and rarely saw it on foot.

Despite the shooting, we hastily ventured up an alleyway, dashing from building to building. Maria was a lot quicker than me - being well practised at stepping over rubble, and not having the inconvenience and weight of a helmet and flak-jacket. She seemed determined to show me something. Upon entering the remains of a burnt out house half way up a hill that faced the Croatian lines, I was confronted by the charred bodies of what were, judging by the remains of their clothes, two elderly people. There weren't many flies but the stench was overpowering in the summer heat. It appeared the old couple, overcome by smoke and unable to escape as their home burned, had just accepted death and lain down and died together. Maria said,

'Look, look, this is what we have to live in.'

Despite the smell of the decomposing corpses, I instinctively took her in my arms and held her close and with tear filled eyes stared down at the blackened decomposing bodies. Maria, for the first time since Ahmići, had awoken both my compassion and emotions, albeit temporarily.

We soon made our way back down the alleyway and returned to the doorstep where we sat previously, this time holding hands. The war continued with the sound of the rat-tat-tat short bursts of light machine guns, interspersed with heavy burst of cannon and incoming and outgoing shells and mortar fire. Quite suddenly, above the noise, I heard a whoosh sound that alerted my senses, closely followed by a bang, which momentarily shook the earth. We both dived headlong for the ground - no time to get into cover. A rocket had slammed into the building next to where trucks were still unloading, closely followed by another. Both impacts were only some forty-five yards away. Small pieces of debris fell from the sky on and around us, as we lay huddled next to each other. It was obvious that our location was directly targeted. We raised our heads and shoulders from the ground glancing at each other for comfort. Maria's beautiful long black hair was now covered in dust, as was her pale looking face. I expect I looked much the same. Then, as the reverberation of the explosion subsided, our attention was drawn to a young woman emerging from the dust, running down the street screaming, before collapsing on the ground with her arms and legs flailing uncontrollably. In other circumstances, I would have been amused at such an unusual sight. Maria and I lay still in the road, watching impassively, neither intending to offer assistance. I looked at Maria and felt that she had seen it all before. The compassion that I previously demonstrated, only minutes before when viewing the bodies of the dead elderly people, had clearly gone. The woman turned out to be our Global Relief Organisation Translator - her nerve had gone - she couldn't take any more. Shortly after, other Global Relief Organisation staff, risking their own lives, carried her kicking and screaming back into cover. I have to ask myself were my emotions, when with Maria and the old dead couple genuine? On the other hand, was I just trying to show a human face to yet another tragedy: to impress her to gain further affection? Maria and I stood up and hugged, unsure of whether we would see each other again.

After some six hours in Mostar, the convoy headed for home. In that time, I had grown quite fond of Maria and we both wanted to keep in touch, if only as friends. For eighteen months or so, we wrote to each other, via the local Red Cross Messaging Service - a blessing to those separated by war. I really didn't expect to see her again but in May 1995 I managed a brief visit to Mostar whilst on my way to Zagreb, in Croatia. Amazingly, I found her home intact. She recognised me straight away and was overcome by emotion. I had only a few minutes; gave her one hundred Deutchemarks to buy food for herself and family on the Black Market, kissed her goodbye and left.

The Bosnian Croats and Bosnian Muslims ultimately decided to unite as a marriage of convenience, combining their military strength to fight the common enemy - the Serbs. Mostar, although largely destroyed and bearing little resemblance to its historical past was at last peaceful and, theoretically, once more one city, albeit with an underlying bitterness between the two sides that is still present to this day.

The translator left the Global Relief Organisation after the convoy, probably emotionally scarred for life.

Our team continued supplying hospitals and local populations as best as we could with the necessities of life. In September my contract expired, and I reluctantly returned home to 'normality', which for me meant unemployment, despondency and no sense of direction. I did however have my very loving and supportive fiancée, Paula: who had patiently and loyally awaited my return. Was it enough?

Chapter Four

As anticipated, and with no immediate prospects, boredom and despondency quickly set in. I felt that everyone I spoke to was completely ignorant. People seemed shallow and obsessed with western consumerism, pursuing social status through material wealth.

Shops were full. Saturdays seemed to be a mad frenzy of people filling shopping trolleys with disposable pre-packed products from brightly illuminated shelves. Adults appeased screaming children with sweets and chocolates whilst waiting in supermarket queues.

My mind frequently wandered back to the ragged children of Bosnia who had never seen sweets or chocolate. I thought how ungrateful these children were: but what were they to know? They were entirely innocent. I soon felt completely alienated in such an environment and tried to find peace by taking long walks in the countryside that surrounded my home. However, hills, ridges, trees, and open spaces invoked sinister feelings of vulnerability. I remained aware and alert to the threat of snipers, mines, and ambush killing zones - although I knew there was no such threat. I began to quarrel with Paula over nothing as I secretly blamed her for me having to return home. I felt uncomfortable in this *country and everything it offered me. I wanted to return to **my** war in Bosnia. A country where a ballpoint pen and a piece of paper to write on, was as important to them as the latest cell phone is to Americans or Western Europeans.*

After being home for a month and making life for Paula positively unpleasant, due to my unreasonable, inflexible attitude and mood swings, the Home Office approached me with a view to working for them, as part of the United Kingdom Convoy Team. If I was to agree, I was to work under the auspices of the United Nations. After using all my uncompromising powers of influence, Paula reluctantly agreed to my return to the war. On reflection, I now realise I bullied her in to agreeing. She knew I had to go and would follow my convictions anyway. Even though she loved me, I was immune to what I was once again asking her to endure. It was always more difficult for those left behind having only the television news coverage to give them an insight into what was happening in a war. It is only bad news that makes good news: television news bulletins did not provide Paula with any comfort and I did little to reassure her, being too wrapped up in my own selfish desires.

I quite plainly was not worthy of the love and devotion that she had shown towards me. Shortly after I went back to Bosnia, she found the strength to end our relationship. This was something that I perhaps should have done some time previously but hadn't the strength to do. A legacy from of my tormented youth? I needed someone to love me - even from afar... Some would say its better that way.

Nothing would stop me from going to where I had found amongst other things happiness and a sense of well-being. I was incredibly self-absorbed - in my own little exhilarating war with my own group of friends. It was exciting, dangerous, unpredictable and at that time, generally good to be part of. My colleagues and I, for the most part thoroughly enjoyed ourselves. I felt like I was in heaven, even though it was nearer to hell; my senses were alert and my face often beamed with obvious contentment. Here I could make good all those previous years of despondency and satisfy all the emotional deficits that were prominent as I grew up. In war, I found the camaraderie and sense of belonging I desperately yearned. The inherent risks of the war didn't really enter my daily thoughts. On one occasion, I didn't contact Paula for two weeks, leaving her in total dismay. I can offer no justification; suffice to say I was irresponsible and too busy satisfying my own needs and feeding an over inflated ego.

I miss her now and after a number of failed relationships have often wondered what would, or should have become of us. Despite this, I had to go and have no regrets about returning to the war.

I landed at Zagreb Airport in Croatia to be met by three fellow Brits who had been sent to pick me up. We were to travel down the coast to Medjurečje in southern Croatia to where I was to initially work from. The other three had been in Croatia for some time and seemed to be enjoying that unique friendship that only war brings. After loading my luggage and whilst leaving the airport car park, one of the team, a mechanic, shouted,

'Stop! - I want that,' 'that' being a large pick up truck,

'I want one of those fuckers to put me tool box in.'

We duly stopped and, within a minute or so, the 'fucker', a five-litre Chevrolet burst into life and we had an addition to the fleet, albeit a stolen one! I smiled in agreement at the eccentricity of needing a very large American pick up truck to put a toolbox in and snuggled down into my seat for the long drive ahead, immediately feeling quite at home.

I was soon to learn that the theft and swapping of vehicles between expatriates was commonplace, although this was the only time I actually saw it happen. We became victims when the Serbs stole one of our trucks. They camouflaged it and put it into military service. After investigation, the UN Military Police located it; the Serbs refusing to give it back unless we paid ten thousand Deutchemarks for its return. They said they had spent considerable time servicing and repairing it, replacing many parts and that they considered this a reasonable price! I wish we had had the same success obtaining parts as they apparently did, for our vehicles were often unroadworthy for lack of spares. The 'ransom' wasn't paid and, under threat from the local UN garrison, the truck was returned to us. A couple of days later I returned to the depot at Zagreb.

This gave me the opportunity to compare the equipment and organisation between the Global Relief Organisation and the United Nations. The UN operated on military lines and had a distinctive military ethos and structure. This wasn't surprising as everyone I encountered had some sort of military background. The managers were ex Captains or Majors, the convoy leaders Sergeants and above. I quite warmed to this, after having spent five years in a Royal Engineers Field Support Squadron TA.

In the transport yard, there were about twenty vehicles that had been either damaged in road accidents, or quite simply shot up. This area was appropriately known as the 'graveyard'. One drizzly evening before being allocated a vehicle, I wandered alone, inspecting the carcasses of the numerous wrecked vehicles. They were now used as a useful cache of much needed spares. A chill swept through my body as I viewed one truck that was similar to the one I would be driving - the cab having been completely riddled with bullets. I tried to imagine what it must have been like for the driver, dying in this way. Blood was clearly splattered all over the inside of the drivers cab. I don't suppose he would have known much about it, but I expect there would have been a few tense moments as he realised what was about to happen; that is if he ever did.

Was I his replacement? Was this what I had to look forward to? For a moment, I felt alone and fearful about what I was doing. This was going to be hazardous but I had no doubt that I would cope, I told myself. Anyway, there was no way that I would go home and lose face - no matter what.

I had been told about a convoy of British trucks that had been ambushed on a mountain pass by a heavy volume of small arms fire. The fire wasn't accurate but several drivers were instantly wounded in their cabs, others scrambled out and took cover beside their trucks. The convoy leader, putting himself in extreme danger, quickly drove back into the 'killing zone' rescuing the wounded and other drivers. By now, the volume of fire had subsided to the odd burst. It was, however, a miracle that he himself wasn't hit. Perhaps the perpetrators of the ambush thought they had done enough or quite simply wanted to immobilise the convoy. The vehicles were abandoned to the attacking force.

Here in the transport yard water tankers, peppered with holes, were parked up lame. They were intended, and initially used to transport water into Sarajevo. This wasn't at all successful and the idea abandoned as most of the water was deposited on the roads en-route, leaving just a few precious gallons left at the bottom of the tank along with the spent bullets. I once again contemplated the fate that I had volunteered for, as I looked around the graveyard at the 'dead' trucks. Was I going to find the same level of companionship with my new colleagues as I had the Global Relief Organisation, I hoped so.

The Leyland DAF trucks that operated from Zagreb were very well equipped for the task in hand. They were originally designed for UN relief work in Africa, but had been diverted to the much more news worthy cause in the Former Yugoslavia. The trucks had heightened and strengthened suspension, good storage for tools, and a differential lock on all three of their axles and four forty-five gallon diesel tanks, which proved most useful, as one or more would often be punctured by bullets. The mechanics were always ready with solder to repair the tanks upon our return. Windscreens often needed repair or replacement - smashed by rock throwing youths and those hostile to the UN mission.

Eventually, the cabs were fitted with protective mesh over the screens and windows, but nothing could be done to protect the fuel tanks. Fortunately, diesel is extremely difficult to ignite and since there were four tanks the puncturing of one or more posed little problem.

In late November 1993, I arrived alone in Tuzla, delivering a brand new Land Rover loaded with army ration packs for the contingent based there. The journey from Medjurečje to Tuzla was quite perilous. I had to join armed UN military convoys for protection in unstable areas; occasionally seeking refuge for a few days at a time at a UN base, waiting for the next scheduled convoy. I often ignored the advice given and, using maps I carried, make my way over the icy mountainous routes alone. In retrospect, this was an extremely dangerous undertaking: hungry, armed militia would have thought nothing of ambushing and killing me, quite simply for the Land Rover and the food I was carrying. I was to live and work from Tuzla, joining a team whose primary task was to distribute food from the warehouse in Tuzla to the even less fortunate people of Zeneca, both besieged cities of industrial significance in

Bosnia. I settled in quickly to the new routine and felt quite at home with my new colleagues.

In addition to siege conditions, Zeneca hosted an uncompromising force of Islamic fundamentalist mercenaries from the Middle East. They were fighting against the perceived or actual Serbian aggression. Not only did they prove to be very courageous and effective fighters, they were feared by the Serbs. The Muslim population of Zeneca also seemed to fear them.

Some of the fundamentalists, in accordance with their historical values and tradition, were insistent that the largely 'westernised' women of Zeneca should cover up their bodies completely, walk behind their men folk, and not display any sign of affection in public. In summer, many of the Muslim women would sunbathe defiantly on the banks of the River Bosna that ran through Zeneca, regardless of the occasional sight of dead bloated bodies, and sometimes whole families passing by - carried along by the gentle current. Mercenaries would often order them to dress and return indoors. Again, in accordance with tradition, and where possible when leaving home, they were expected to wear a yashmak, (traditional Muslim dress and veil whereby only the eyes are exposed) when outdoors. These values originating from their homelands where it was normal and perfectly acceptable, did not sit comfortably with the majority of women in Zeneca.

Tuzla was the second largest city of Bosnia and home to a major chemical plant. The Serbs were desperate to take control of it and surrounded the city. They hoped to break the morale of the people by shelling or starving them into submission. History has previously proved this tactic ineffective. The will of a subdued people is usually strengthened by such hardship. The London blitz and the allied bombing of Berlin in World War II, being prime examples of such strength and defiance in the face of adversity: both peoples remained resolute in defence. Tuzla was out of range of snipers but not artillery, and, despite numerous deaths from shelling, proved to be considerably safer than the besieged capital of Bosnia - Sarajevo.

The local inhabitants unfortunately received nothing from us, but those pouring in from overrun towns and villages did. The primary task of the UN was to assist refugees but not the desperate and often deprived local population. I felt that this was unrealistic and potentially explosive, causing tension amongst the famished original population of Tuzla, who could openly see the refugees getting considerable assistance. The locals had to rely on help from non-government agencies, such as the Global Relief Organisation, Medicin Sans Frontier and Care International and numerous other private organisations. The displaced received help from both government and non-government providers. The tension was to finally explode one mid-week afternoon, when the locals overran our warehouse and stole everything - they were literally starving. I sat on top of my truck cab and let them get on with it. They meant me no harm and anyway I sympathised with them. It was nonetheless a little unnerving as the crowd of people burst open the locked gate to the entrance of the compound and stormed up the drive. The top of my lorry cab didn't offer any protection.

After this, the Swedish Army permanently guarded our civilian UN base with an armoured personnel carrier mounting a heavy machine gun, pointing menacingly at the gates. The Swedes would not have had the authority or the will to fire upon these hungry unarmed people, if they again chose to overrun the compound. Nevertheless, they did indeed look threatening and kept the locals at bay.

There were five drivers, a convoy leader and two mechanics, all British, based in Tuzla. We lived in a reasonably comfortable local hotel, renting the whole of the seventh floor, along with a permanent armed guard. We often had running water and sometimes electricity. I had my own room facing the Serb lines some two miles away. This wasn't a problem as sniping wasn't a threat and the chance of being hit by stray rounds from fighting taking place in the nearby hills, at that range was, I considered, negligible. Shelling of the city, however, was always a threat, but nowhere near as much as in other enclaves, such as Srebrnica and Sarajevo.

American F-16 fighters patrolled the skies overhead, performing aerobatics, which delighted us as onlookers. The locals rarely paid much attention. The F-16s did not, however, deter the occasional daring strike by Serbian ground attack aircraft that would fly in extremely low - under ground based radar - drop their bombs and make their escape before anyone realised what had happened. This left utter panic, burning buildings, along with numerous dead and injured. With all the advanced technology available to the Americans, I often wondered how relatively old unsophisticated Serbian Mig Fighter-Bombers were able to penetrate the supposed protective screen (no fly zone) offered by British, American and French aircraft.

I enjoyed living in Tuzla, despite the winter of 1993/94 being bitterly cold. Minus twenty and a wind chill factor of minus thirty degrees Celsius in the mountains not at all uncommon. The chilly wintry conditions would seriously inhibit our ability to operate - vehicles froze up and refused to start. A number of aid personnel had died from exposure whilst attempting to traverse some of Bosnia's most mountainous regions during the winter period.

Early on, after my arrival there were ample supplies of boxed army rations, we would take it in turns to cook breakfast in the mechanics' workshop. When not on convoy, we passed the time maintaining the trucks and watching very poor quality locally obtained videos. Along with my colleagues, I often drank what seemed like pure alcohol with Bosnian Muslim soldiers, in simple underground bars and dugouts. Drinking had by now become not only a coping mechanism but helped alleviate long periods of boredom as a lot of time was spent just hanging around, washing off the trucks, performing routine maintenance and that sort of thing. Another favourite, more engaging pastime, was scrounging or stealing from the nearby Norwegian and Swedish UN Army bases for anything that would be of any conceivable use to us.

On one occasion after negotiating the fifty miles of mountainous pathways and roads from Tuzla to Zeneca, we unloaded our supplies at the warehouse and 'Big M', the convoy leader, told us that he needed two of us to go over to the United Nations Headquarters at Kiseljak - located thirty-five miles south of Zeneca. We were to pick up a parcel for him. I jumped at the chance, as did the other driver, who was sent with me. We had heard the Headquarters staff lived very well indeed in the former purpose-built 1984 Olympic athletes' accommodation.

Upon arrival, forgetting why we were there, we headed straight for the Officers' Mess, which, as UN civilian staff we were allowed to use. After persuading the disbelieving well-dressed Duty Officer of our UN status, despite our unshaven, dirty, and generally scruffy appearance, the Duty Officer reluctantly allowed us in. We looked at each other in amazement - we lived primarily on our army ration packs and breakfasts cooked on a wood-burning stove.

The general staff here at Kiseljak had pork, beef, chicken, an abundance of fruit and vegetables, salad served in a buffet-style arrangement and fresh milk, all flown in daily by helicopter. We didn't speak, looked at each other in amazement grabbed and ate all we could, savouring the unexpected moment of luxury. We filled our pockets with fruit and savoury snacks. A large joint of beef taken from the carvery found its way into my utility bag - something to share with the lads later - if it got that far. The catering staff didn't care - I think they understood. Ironically, less than thirty miles away, the inhabitants of Zeneca to the north, and the inhabitants of Sarajevo to the east, were slowly but positively starving to death. We completed our task and returned to share what was left of our booty with our colleagues.

Whilst in Tuzla, we were allowed ten minutes per week use of the satellite telephone, which was provided for us to maintain contact with home and liaise with Headquarters in Zagreb. This was in addition to the high frequency radio sets carried in our vehicles, which could somehow also be used to link up with the home UK telephone network. Drivers would often call home when on convoy - presuming the right atmospheric conditions prevailed.

Initially, I would log every minute's use of the satellite phone, but soon came to realise that no one really cared how long the call lasted - the privilege was routinely abused. A quiet eye was turned to our misdemeanour, as one-hour telephone calls home became quite normal.

Our trucks were very old, ex army Bedford four ton trucks. We had five, but barely managed to keep three, sometimes four, serviceable. Surprisingly, spare parts were difficult to obtain from England, which necessitated the mechanics performing miracles through a process of cannibalisation and ingenuity and the odd part that reached us from the graveyard in Zagreb.

As time passed and we became more settled in Tuzla, relationships began to form with local girls. Some of the team were happily married and remained completely faithful to their partners. Others evidently found it difficult to avoid interacting with young women who sought our attention. The girlfriend of one of the team members had given him a box containing over one hundred condoms, saying,

'I know you will sleep around, but at least use these.' He did sleep around and never used them.

The locals had already endured two and a half years of war in siege conditions. Adult women were willing to sleep with foreign nationals to find love and comfort and gain favour, thus giving them access to items such as clean water, soap, chocolate, jam, and bread. The vain hope of escaping under the illusion of a passport out of this hell must also have been in their minds. Cynically, I sometimes thought it as prostitution in a most basic form: although I knew of at least one aid worker who married a girl from Bosnia, taking her home to the UK.

I was not completely immune to the temptation of local women, morality temporarily taking a back seat to the need for sexual gratification and emotional comfort - for both of us. However, just as at home, I never sustained a relationship for long. I once spent a whole evening drinking with and chatting up a very attractive freelance reporter working for one of the well-known broadsheets. Unfortunately, my advances were rejected, I got so drunk at a local bar that by the time we got back to her apartment with sex very much on both our minds I simply passed out whilst kissing her. She left me on the couch fully clothed and went to bed in disgust! I didn't let on to the lads that I had blown it with one of the most desirable women in Tuzla at that time.

However, there was a young girl, twenty-one years old, whom I became close to and had some feelings for. She offered me a temporary escape from the war. She liked me to call her Anna, the only western name she knew. She was an attractive Serbian girl with Turkish features and shoulder length black hair, living in a city of Muslims. Like many Serbs living in Muslim areas, she was accepted without fear of repression. The Muslims were far more tolerant than other ethnic groups. Her English was poor, but better than my Serbo-Croat. I would often share some of my evenings with her and her family, when not on convoy. They had a very small apartment of three rooms - a living room, kitchen, and one bedroom. Her family often left Anna and myself alone whilst we made love. Under the circumstances and knowing it wouldn't last we made the best of the short time we spent together. I guess it was all a bit crude but we both found a respite from the war when alone together. The apartment housed her mother, father, grandparents and younger sister and brother. Anna's sister, who was fifteen years old, baked bread at an army bakery. She worked twelve hours per day and was rewarded with a loaf at the end of a shift and a pint of cooking oil on Sundays, that being the going rate at the time.

Anna showed me a photograph of herself before the war, when she was a student in Belgrade, Serbia, studying music. She was now almost unrecognisable, like her sister, so much thinner and gaunt after three years of mild but persistent malnutrition. She was always hungry and looked forward to the food that I acquired for her and her family.

The apartment was very cramped, but at least they had shelter. The whole family was incredibly thin and hadn't any money. I willingly shared my army supplies of food with them. We had a considerable store of tinned steak, which proved very popular. As UN staff could use the nearby Swedish and Norwegian Army base canteens, I was occasionally able to bring some fruit. A rare treat indeed, as all were perishable foodstuffs. One evening, I took a couple of bananas for Anna's little brother. When I gave one to him, he stared at it looking quite bewildered; then took a large bite out of one without peeling the skin off. Anna laughed and explained that he had never seen bananas before. He was four years old. My mind briefly wandered back to the kids back home and the supermarket queues. His mother placed her hands over her face and started to cry, saying she had not seen a banana since the beginning of the war. Sniffling, she took it from him, carefully peeled it, handing it back to his expectant little hands. The rest were cut up under candlelight, whilst every member of the family watched in keen anticipation, awaiting their small share. It was a real treat for them and quite pitiful for me to witness. What child in Western Europe hadn't seen a banana by the time he was four years old?

A local youth of fourteen latched onto us when we were at our workshops. He spoke excellent English without any of the routine slang and swearing that was prevalent among us. He sought acceptance and truly found it. His father was dead and he became the 'man' of his family at this young age. His association with us enabled him to provide items for his family that were unobtainable to most Bosnians in Tuzla. Ben, as we called him, (I never knew his real name) became our official 'scrounger'. He knew the Black Market very well and, for a small fee, would get us almost anything we needed. We fed and clothed him, in return for his services washing the trucks, dishes and doing any odd jobs that we could persuade him to do.

It was always Ben's friendly face that welcomed us back from convoys, often with stolen or bought booty (he got paid anyway) that we had asked him to find. I often wonder what became of Ben when we left, but I am sure he survived the war on his cunning and wit alone.

Periodically, we would take supplies to refugee camps situated high up in the hills around Tuzla. These camps held refugees who had been displaced early on in the war; looking semi-permanent. There was row upon row of World War II Nissan corrugated type huts, neatly laid out on an excavated plateau. The interior of the huts were partitioned with plastic sheeting, providing *some* privacy and a space of approximately ten feet by ten feet for each family. A narrow corridor ran down the middle of the huts linking together the 'rooms'. Outside, there was a row of wood burning stoves, providing both hot water and cooking facilities - an excellent choice, as there was an abundance of wood nearby from both living and fallen trees.

Children played in the thick snow and took great delight in the snowball fights that we initiated on our arrival. They seemed well fed and oblivious to the war that was taking place around them. It was an uplifting experience to see them enjoying themselves. For the adults it was a different story. Most of them had had their homes destroyed and knew there was little hope of ever going home. They understood only too well that their future was one of further misery and strife. We provided some contact with the outside world and, if nothing else, a feeling that they had not been completely abandoned.

Another trip I particularly enjoyed whilst based in Tuzla, was to the Bihać pocket, a small Bosnian Muslim controlled town situated in the new self-proclaimed Republika of Srbska. They were completely surrounded by Serbs and fighting hard for their very existence and indeed, the right to live. They were in absolute fear; the Serbs were determined to rout the Bosnians and declare the town as a 'Muslim free zone'. Kenyan United Nations troops were stationed nearby for their protection. I welcomed their hospitality when we visited Bihać, staying at their base. In fact, they were probably the friendliest people I have ever met and excellent soldiers.

Equipped with mostly ex British Army equipment and despite gaining independence from the United Kingdom in 1966, they were surprisingly pro British: asking many questions about what they still, seemingly, considered their Motherland. I spent many evenings with the Kenyan troops, regularly attending their prayer and hymn service; thoroughly enjoying listening to them singing in Swahili, their native language - sharing their traditional food. They had an inherent belief in the good in all men and were a complete delight to be with; all spoke very good English. The Kenyan United Nations contingent consisted of soldiers from many different tribes who had grown up in what I had always imagined to be 'typical' African villages. I was fascinated to hear about their families and life in Africa. It was a truly cultural experience and one of my more refined and educational encounters in Bosnia.

I was due to take some leave and had a strange feeling that I wouldn't be coming back. Before leaving Tuzla for good, I filled my large black holdall with food I had acquired from the nearby army bases or from our stores. I set off on foot one night, after curfew, in complete darkness, hauling my booty across the city so that Anna and her family would have something to eat. Whilst I was walking, shells began to fall intermittently - my pace quickened. After some very close impacts I sought cover under a viaduct. The twenty-five minute walk subsequently took an hour and a half, but nevertheless I arrived safely with only a dull (and quite normal) ringing in my ears. The family, whom I would never see again, was most grateful. They once again shared my offerings amongst themselves. Mother took control of most of it, storing some away, knowing that there was little chance of there being more in such abundance. I shared no tears with Anna and no promises were made. We had provided emotional comfort for each other, and now, in my typical cold, indifferent manner, decided it was time to cut any emotional ties: leaving her to whatever fate was to befall her - and Tuzla. The consequences for Anna were dire should it fall into Serbian hands - it never did.

Chapter Five

When able to fulfil our primary task of delivering aid, it was not uncommon for our convoys to return with bullet holes in the trucks; luck was with us - or so we thought. Several drivers had already been wounded; some severely, but none killed. Indeed, the Norwegians, whom we had previously shared a base with in Zagreb, had already suffered twelve fatalities. Their flag always seemed to fly at half-mast.

In January 1994 whilst I was taking leave, luck ran out for my small team of five drivers. Three of them were hijacked, and subsequently shot, killing one in an execution style encounter with extremists.

Paul Goodall had recently joined us in Tuzla, from one of the other teams based in Medjurečje, Southern Croatia, from where I had briefly stayed and transferred from some months earlier. Paul had left the British Army, after nine years service with the Royal Engineers. He had seen action in the Gulf as a Section Commander, being one of the first units to breach Iraqi defences, whilst under hostile artillery fire; thus allowing British Armoured Infantry units to pass through unhindered by static defences, once the land offensive began.

Paul told me of the difficulties he had coming to terms with shooting dead an Iraqi soldier - who was surrendering. The soldier, who turned out to be a Sergeant, and other Iraqis' walked towards the dugout occupied by Paul and his squad. All but the Sergeant were weaponless and had their hands in the air. The Sergeant was still carrying his AK47 Machine Gun. Paul took aim with his 7.62mm Self-Loading Rifle; the Sergeant continued to walk towards him, his weapon by his side. Then, for no apparent reason, the Sergeant raised his gun in Paul's direction. Paul fired two shots into his chest, killing him instantly. The other Iraqis' fell to the floor, begging for mercy, whilst expecting to be shot. No more shots were fired: Paul and his squad cautiously moved forward securing the rest of the prisoners.

It transpired that the Sergeant was offering his weapon as a gesture of surrender, an Arabic custom. Many Iraqis' were to lose their lives in similar circumstances, due to the ignorance of coalition forces. Paul was a compassionate man and told me that this incident haunted him, and that he suffered frequent nightmares. At the time, he informed his Commanding Officer of the incident who had quite simply told him to 'forget it.' It wasn't so easy for someone such as Paul, being a sensitive man, to dismiss the loss of human life, regardless of the circumstances.

Paul was a likeable fellow: sharing many common interests, we quickly became good friends. He was a selfless man and prior to leaving Sarajevo, whilst en-route to Tuzla, had helped a woman whom he had met professionally. She hadn't seen her daughter since the war began and feared for her safety. She gave Paul ten Deutchemarks ($4), all she had, which was more than one month's average salary at the time, asking that he find her daughter in Tuzla and give her the money. Paul promised he would.

Paul and I found the address, an apartment above a cafeteria: one of many serving thick black sludge masquerading as coffee. Instead of giving the daughter ten Deutchemarks, Paul made it up to one hundred; casually mentioning it was from her mother. This was typical of Paul who sadly lost his life on 27th January 1994.

I felt privileged to be invited to Paul's funeral, which took place in a small stone chapel, set in the rolling hills near his hometown in

Yorkshire. It was a cold grey day, befitting the event. Paul's wife, children, and parents attended - no press. Silently, I lowered my head and hid my grief but to this day have an uncomfortable feeling of 'survivor's guilt'. Paul had children and family responsibilities. I did not.

Paul's parents quickly learned of our history and asked me what it was really like in Bosnia. I was lost for words, I didn't know what Paul had told them and didn't want to contradict anything he had said. I struggled to get my words out.

'I guess it was like any other war,' I said. Not knowing what else I could say to parents who had just lost a son. The war for me was sometimes very confusing, uncertain, inhuman, ruthless and beyond comprehension to anyone who wasn't there - but I didn't tell them that.

We were often very coy in describing the war, for fear of upsetting relatives and friends. Up until this day, I was still enjoying many aspects of it. Now it was different. A wife without a husband; children without a father; parents without a son. This was something in my relative immaturity I hadn't had to think about before. All of us stood next to the grave with tears in our eyes and empty, drawn faces. My boyhood illusions of war now utterly shattered. I looked at them in turn with vacant, pathetic eyes.

Instead of going on to answer their questions fully, and by now with only the three of us left standing aside Paul's grave, I began to tell them, in a croaky voice, of Paul's kindness - and his many acts of selflessness. I told of how we had become close friends, sharing many personal confidences, during the short time that we had known each other.

They pleaded with me not to go back - telling me that I was welcome to visit them at any time. I never did: not wanting to remind them or myself of the circumstances of Paul's death.

The day that Paul died started like any other. The convoy departed on time from Tuzla - bound for Zeneca, with a cargo of food and medicine. After the normal radio checks, drivers settled down for the journey ahead. The drive would normally take between eight and ten hours, depending on road conditions and delays at the numerous checkpoints. Most journeys were routine and upon safe arrival at our destination, the trucks would line up outside the warehouse to be unloaded by anxious local staff. It was normal practice for two drivers, usually Paul and myself, to transfer the convoy's personal luggage in the convoy leaders Land Rover and drive to secure accommodation in town. I was not present on this particular convoy, and as there was rather a lot of luggage, 'Big M' - the convoy leader, Adrian, a fellow driver and Paul crammed into the Land Rover; leaving the locally hired workers to carry on unloading the rice, flour, and medical supplies.

Whilst en-route to the hotel, they were waved down and hijacked by what was *believed* to be two gun toting mercenary Mujahadin youths (Islamic fighters to the death), who had aligned themselves to the BiH (Bosnian Muslim Army), but did not accept orders from them. Whether Mujahadin freedom fighters or not, some combatants chose to fight the war on their own terms: with their own rules and values - eliminating infidels (none believers) as they saw fit. This could include Western European international aid workers such as us. The youths, both under twenty years old, one of whom spoke very good English, ordered 'Big M' and the others to drive to a nearby school playground. The three were ordered out of the vehicle and manhandled to their knees. After some discussion between the youths, they were ordered back into the Land Rover, receiving instructions to drive to a nearby river. On arrival, they were told to kneel. This time on the banks of the River Bosna. They had no option but to comply. Some minutes later a Middle Eastern looking man in a smart black civilian suit drove up, got out of his old Mercedes, and drew his pistol from inside his jacket.

Paul, thirty-six years old, a married father and only son, was shot twice in the back of the head, killing him instantly. As the shots that killed Paul rang out, Big M and Adrian attempted to escape by instantly jumping into the icy river; both received gunshot wounds, as the executioner and the youths riddled the icy river with both pistol and machine gun fire. Big M was hit in his back and Adrian in an arm and leg. Both managed to survive the ordeal; making it to the opposite riverbank some way down the river, where they received assistance from local villagers sympathetic to the UN mission. The freezing water slowed down their blood flow, reducing blood loss through their open wounds - slowing down the onset of shock and helping keep them alive. The two survivors were subsequently evacuated to the British UN

Base at Vitez, lucky to escape with their lives: both received emergency medical care. One week later, they were flown home. The Bosnian police later arrested the youths and man who committed this barbarous act: miraculously, and in secure custody they 'escaped.'

Some days later 'unknown forces' reputed to be British Special Forces operating in the area, ambushed the stolen Land Rover and, without mercy, gunned down the occupants. We were shown photographs taken immediately after the incident but unfortunately, Paul's assassin was not one of those killed.

We received assurances from relevant British authorities that Paul's killer would be dealt with in an 'uncompromising manner', regardless of his worldwide location. The British UN contingent would not risk another unnecessary death at the hands of extremists. An example ***had*** to be made.

It is important to note that this was a rare case of extremism perpetrated by fanatics. Throughout my time in Bosnia, I found the overwhelming majority of Muslim people to be friendly, accommodating, and very supportive of our mission. There is good and bad in all men, and war, after all, has a habit of bringing out both the best and worse in people, including myself. Religious beliefs were never an issue. Survival was.

My thoughts are often with Paul and his family. Paul was not just another victim of the war - at that time he was the closest friend I had. To me, all other deaths in Bosnia were nameless victims. Death in the Balkans had more or less become an everyday occurrence, which I largely blanked out of my thoughts. This was a tragedy on a personal level and one that I have yet to completely come to terms with - and possibly never will.

What was going through Paul's mind as his assassin cocked his pistol before firing the two shots into his head? What would any man's thoughts be prior to execution? It plays on my mind and I often daydream the scenario. What would I have done had I been kneeling next to him? What if I had been armed and nearby? I imagined being in close proximity and bravely shooting the gunmen dead to save the lives of my friends, but it wasn't like that. If only I could have done something ...

After this tragic event, our team operating in central Bosnia was ordered to disband; two other teams continued to operate elsewhere.

Shortly after, I terminated my contract driving for the UN, made a couple of local radio interviews upon returning home, and thought my time in conflict zones was well and truly over.

Chapter Six

After eight months working as a sales rep selling bedroom furniture, I was fired for not reaching sales targets - by a long margin. This was in part due to me not bothering to leave home on sunny days, preferring to sunbathe or play snooker in a local pub with a good friend of mine - Dave. Incidentally, he was also a sales rep for a local car parts dealership. We had been friends since our first day of school and like me, cared little for his poorly paid job. Falsifying records and visits to customers became an entertaining game for us both. Unsurprisingly, Dave was also fired a week later - for similar reasons. Nonetheless, we had a great summer!

I detested the job and had no interest in the lies and general falseness that was expected of me in a sales environment. Once again, I felt very out of place and completely alienated in a competitive, commercially driven world. I found myself longing for the opportunity to return to the war and live by values I firmly believed in. Bosnia was a place where I felt confident, strong and comfortably at home: entirely out of the rat race with nothing to worry about, except, of course being killed. Paul's dreadful death was still very much on my mind but I was determined that it wouldn't stand in my way.

Early in 1995, driven by stubborn determination and despite protests from *family* and friends (Dave pleaded with tears in his eyes such was his concern), I returned to Bosnia - once again working for the Global Relief Organisation. An experienced volunteer was urgently needed to go to the besieged city of Sarajevo, the capital city of Bosnia: I had both the experience and utmost desire.

Originally home to some six hundred and eighty thousand people at the outbreak of war, there were now approximately three hundred and forty thousand of the sophisticated, pro-western urban dwellers left. Known as Saralilje (people of Sarajevo), many had already been killed. Others had fled to bordering countries or Italy whilst they could - at the onset of war.

I was to work largely alone, delivering aid to the needy in and around Sarajevo, subsequently overseeing, and becoming responsible for the warehouse stores.

Built in a valley in central Bosnia, Sarajevo reaches out in like a crooked finger for several miles. Ottoman architecture dominates the 'old town' with quaint, low roofed dwellings and cobbled back streets, servicing small shops, cafés, and charming restaurants, tucked away in shaded corners. Away from the old town, the skyline had been ruined by aesthetically distressing concrete blocks - erected by Tito's town planners before the war. They did however, appear culturally modern, helping to attract western finance and credit.

Despite my previous experience of war, I was unexpectedly excited at the prospect of going to work in Sarajevo. It dominated the news and fascinated me. I wanted to be there - a new adventure and in the war proper. I wasn't at all afraid, believing I would survive in my freshly established, and misplaced belief in my own immortality. After all, I had survived danger before - why shouldn't I continue to believe that I was immortal?

Sarajevo was totally surrounded by the Bosnian Serb Army or, as the United Nations amusingly once described it, 'in a state of tactical encirclement'. An understated description of a near hopeless situation, and one for which the combined governments of the West, were in fact, partly to blame.

The prevailing siege conditions made it even more appealing. I was far away from the bureaucratic backstabbing that seemed to exist amongst headquarters staff, based in Zagreb, the Croatian capital. I'm sure it wasn't the case, but to me they appeared to do little more than call meetings and take issue with petty rules. I would rather look out for what is happening around me in the middle of a war zone, and not for a knife in the back of those seeking more responsibility and promotion at the expense of others. Despite this, 'office culture' turned out to be as rife in Sarajevo, as in any office back home. I soon realised that some individuals with whom I worked with in Sarajevo, would do almost anything to enhance the quality of their CV - to impress any potential future employer after the war. In war, and in particular siege conditions, everyone needs and depends on each other - leaving very little room for anything else. I liked and used to take comfort from that simple understanding, never really coming to terms with the mentality of a small number of my colleagues.

I was met at Sarajevo Airport by Global Relief Organisation staff and climbed into the back of an armoured Land Rover; apparently, it wasn't healthy to hang around. It was late February and the bouts of winter fog that provided cover from snipers were ending - just as I arrived. No longer could the condemned citizens of Sarajevo feel any measure of safety offered by freezing early morning fog - that often hung over the now faceless and scarred city. We hurried through the checkpoints leading off the airport on a road known as the 'Blue Road.' The Blue Road was under the constant observation of Serb snipers who, I was later to learn, shot anyone; aid workers, journalists, soldiers, civilians alike, whenever they liked - it was that easy. I suspect that to them it was something akin to shooting game on an African Safari, or just something to do to break the monotony of siege warfare. Indeed, at a later date, a poorly aimed rocket-propelled grenade was to pass between the rear of the truck in front of me and my truck - whilst on the Blue Road. A considerable escalation of aggression compared to sniper fire. This clearly demonstrated just how dangerous travelling on the Blue Road could be. Evidently fired from nearby Serb positions the rocket exploded harmlessly in a nearby, hopefully, unoccupied building. Designed to penetrate light armoured tanks, it would have decimated the cab of my truck along with me. A sobering thought indeed.

My first impression of Sarajevo was of drab, communist-style concrete, burnt out buildings, bereft of life and colour. Bullet ridden walls, broken glass, tattered and torn curtains blew gently in the breeze: a far cry from 1984, when the city buzzed with life; hosting the Winter Olympics at the Zetra Stadium in the city centre where English ice skaters Torville and Dean won their gold medal. The collapsed Olympic Stadium now housed Swedish UN troops. The nearby grounds that once hosted field events were already overflowing with freshly dug graves, bearing plain wooden markers; inscribed with only a name and date of death. I looked over the thousands of silent graves whilst imagining the tens of thousands of spectators that once surrounded these very fields, shouting and cheering, as sporting records were broken and medals won. Were some of the people who had been watching the games back in 1984 now buried here? Probably.

The streets were mostly empty, apart from a few women and children, scurrying around overturned cars, burnt out buses and bins. I caught the occasional sight of hunched backs, stooped low in the trenches that linked apartments together. They carried plastic containers, searching for water, a battle in itself. Many had already died from a sniper's bullet, seeking this most basic human need. On one occasion, from the safety of my nearby armoured Land Rover, I saw a skinny youth of about fourteen years wearing a green duffle coat emerge from a trench, to take a short cut back to his apartment. He was carrying a 'Jerrycan' type container. Quite suddenly, in conjunction with a loud crack, he was thrown mercilessly back into the trench as a sniper's bullet impacted into his body. No twitching, and seemingly very little blood: a straight clean kill. Good shot you evil bastard, I callously and coldly thought, subconsciously gaining comfort from the Kevlar armour that surrounded me. Seconds later a girl of a similar age, wearing a dirty black skirt and grey jacket scuttled along the trench, reached over the parapit and, with one hand, carefully retrieved the water container. She then hastily stepped over the body of the youth and continued along the trench, apparently unconcerned by the risk, not even glancing at the dead boy. Her only concern was to get precious water.

The only civilian men I saw were usually disabled and on crutches. Probably crippled as a result of stepping on anti-personnel mines. I also noticed the occasional Bosnian police or army patrol - nervously patrolling the streets. A startling one million mines were subsequently laid around Sarajevo and the disputed suburbs. This caused untold misery, not only to the combatants, but also to blameless civilians, many of whom were women and children. Numerous remain in place to this day, indirectly prohibiting the re-population of many once vibrant pre-war villages near to Sarajevo.

I had quickly learned it was frighteningly unsafe to allow yourself be exposed on the city's streets, particularly during daylight hours. Snipers actively sought new targets. I was an equally good proposition once in their sights - as was anyone caught in the open, during their working day.

Tank traps made from iron girders and welded together, in an upright position, littered entrances to side roads. I noticed the body of a middle-aged looking man slumped over one of them - nobody had moved him. It was unusual, as I understood it to be a Muslim tradition to bury their war dead before sunset on the day of death. Maybe he had no family, or maybe no one thought it was worth the risk collecting the now disintegrating remains...

We sped on flat out through the streets of the Blue Route to our headquarters, dodging concrete slabs and other obstacles that were once barricades from previous street battles.

Newspapers, plastic sheeting, and litter skipped in the wind down the near empty streets. Starving dogs foraged amongst the many piles of rubbish that had accumulated since the beginning of war. Never before had I witnessed such an eerie, unfathomably surreal scene. Graffiti on the wall next to the Global Relief Organisation Headquarters read in English 'Welcome to Hell'. I began to feel that I was in fact at hell's door; once again wondering what would become of me in the next few months...

I used the Blue Route regularly during the coming months, adopting a sinister, almost scientific interest in watching the body on the tank trap undergo the process of decomposition. Initially, flies buzzed around his gaping mouth, feeding on his internals before moving onto his now leathered, blackened skin: maggots emerged from every orifice, eating the flesh until it was nothing more than a skeleton clothed in faded green army fatigues. It was quite a morbid but nevertheless interesting scientific spectacle.

The Head of Assignment soon briefed me on the hidden dangers of the city: sniping, shelling, and mortars all daily occurrences. It was totally forbidden to travel in anything other than an armoured vehicle (which we had plenty) and advisable, where possible, to remain in cover - preferably away from windows.

Although predominantly of Belgian origin, the staff were of many different nationalities. There was a Swedish water engineer, a German truck driver, a nurse from New Zealand and a French-Canadian sanitation specialist (who later married a local girl, whom I understand was already married to a Canadian!). There were also several Dutch Nationals, bringing the total number of Global Relief Organisation staff to around twenty-two. Working alongside us, fifteen or so locally employed personnel, two of whom completed all the administration tasks pertaining to the warehousing and distribution.

The unemotional, no nonsense approach I adapted to any task in hand, and apparent lack of empathy displayed at times of bereavement, quickly earned me the reputation of being an insensitive bastard - albeit a fair one, as Alma, the elder of the two secretaries, would often remind me. This underlined my inexperience and immaturity in dealing with emotions associated in coping with death (and other emotions) at that time.

Whenever I went into their office in the morning, asking how they were, it was not uncommon for either of them to jest.

'The natives are fine, awaiting your orders Sir.' In time, I learned the importance of showing compassion towards my colleagues, that I did in fact feel.

The Belgians, although very professional, were elitist and kept themselves pretty much to themselves. I always associated them with a certain aloofness, which marked their assumed, self-importance and supposed status. Whenever a new member of staff of Belgian origin arrived, they were given the best accommodation and an invitation from the Head of Assignment (herself later to be wounded by shrapnel) and

Deputy Head, to their rented house for a meal. This was never the case for new non-Belgian personnel who also worked in the field - in equal danger. Field staff were often in more danger than colleagues working in the solidly constructed headquarters in Sarajevo. Hans, the other truck driver and I felt somewhat neglected, we never received an invitation. Despite this, both the Head of Assignment and her deputy were very approachable professional people, completely dedicated to their task.

At our disposal, for the distribution of supplies were four armoured trucks and trailers. The truck could carry ten tonnes and the trailer eight. Due to an oversight by whoever was responsible for ordering the vehicles, someone with limited knowledge of the haulage industry I presume, had inadvertently made it difficult to load them to maximum capacity. All flights into Sarajevo came with pallets made in the European Community. This made it difficult trying to fit the larger 'euro pallets' onto the back of trucks that were not in fact designed to take them. It would often necessitate breaking one or more of the loaded pallets down; wasting time, manpower and effort trying to make them fit.

It was normal practice for both Hans and I to keep the same truck. Mine had the call sign Yankee Golf 416, shortened to '416' on the radio. This was nothing more than a shortening of the Belgian number plate. It wasn't absolutely necessary for us to keep the same lorries, but we personalised them and preferred it that way. I put a large white toy furry seal in my cab window, this being the first thing sometimes-hostile guards at checkpoints would see. I also wrapped a flak-jacket permanently around the drivers seat; providing a further modicum, or illusion of safety. This was in addition to the protection afforded by the Kevlar-armoured cab - two inches of armoured windscreen, and one-inch armoured side windows completing the package. Strangely, the grill, providing airflow to the radiators on the front of the truck was not armoured. This would cost the Global Relief Organisation dearly as the engine wasn't protected from shrapnel. On one occasion, shrapnel destroyed the main radiator, air conditioning radiator and associated plumbing, completely disabling my truck with just one near miss.

The fluffy white seal was a different kind of added 'psychological' protection, proving useful in breaking the ice with nervous, often tired soldiers at checkpoints. They would point and laugh, making me human and of no threat to them - or indeed their values.

First light every morning was met with a short artillery barrage of mortars and heavy guns - and inevitable reply. Despite some direct hits on my hotel, I eventually learned to sleep through it: often waking up on the floor, not knowing how I had got there; my subconscious having taken over and placing me more safely by the side of the bed.

A total of forty-four million pounds of explosive was dumped on Sarajevo and surrounding villages during the war, much of it during the time I was there. I actually missed the sound of reassuring outgoing and fear-provoking incoming shells, when eventually returning home, finding it difficult to sleep - the quietness was just so unnatural.

Outdoors, it was always important to be aware of the nearest cover taking great care if possible not to expose yourself to known, or probable, sniper locations. 'If you can see their positions, they can see you' was what a Bosnian Army Captain once told me. Undoubtedly, observing this simple common sense rule saved my life. Initially, and despite witnessing the youth being shot in the trench, I rebelled against the idea of scurrying around like a rat - from cover to cover. However, this soon changed as I became further exposed to the total lack of morality displayed by combatants in the Bosnian War. I did indeed end up scurrying around like a rat, always looking for the nearest bolthole when sudden shelling, or frantic firefights erupted.

In the back streets, somewhat sheltered from sniping, I would see people restlessly queuing for bread. Everyone looking nervous, tired, and underfed. Many men had given up shaving, which further enhanced their gaunt, unkempt appearance. They stood pitifully, hands in pockets, heads bowed - broken people.

The locally employed Global Relief Organisation staff I spoke to lived in fear of the surrounding Bosnian Serbian Army overrunning the city. In this eventuality, there was virtually no chance of escaping from incarceration, rape, or premature death. However, the chances of this happening in reality were now beginning to diminish. The defences around the city were becoming stronger by the day and the well-organised Bosnian Muslim Army (BiH) was increasing in strength. Nevertheless, the confines of the city were a crushingly depressing environment to exist in, and one that I, like many others, would take time to recover from.

Outdoor market vendors set out their stalls every Thursday - as they had done for as long as anyone could remember, but it was different now. The usual hustle and bustle associated with outdoor markets simply did not exist. Most people now trudged the market in short steps with staring eyes and bony, hollow faces; searching for the odd 'bargain' they could perhaps afford. Single eggs traded for around $5, a candle for about $7. Apples and potatoes were seldom available and then only to the social elite of Sarajevo, who had not yet spent all of their savings, and having vision, early on in the war, to convert it from the now worthless Bosnian Dinar, into hard currency, preferably the Deutchemark.

Most stalls offered bric-a-brac and treasured, but now worthless, family heirlooms. The starving masses needed food and uncontaminated water, not jewellery.

Pet dogs in Sarajevo had long been put out on the streets, and, along with cats - eaten. People scavenged leaves and grass to add to boiling water, thinly disguised as soup, food was in desperately short supply. I heard a story of a widowed twenty-six year old mother of two infants who, faced with the constant reality of never finding sufficient food to feed both children, allowed one to die; hopefully, securing the life of the other. An incredibly brave decision brought about by sheer desperation and made in the knowledge that the supply of food entering Sarajevo, was likely to deteriorate - despite the newfound strength of the BiH.

Surviving dogs formed packs and roamed the streets. Their foraging of food in the vast piles of stinking disease harbouring rubbish was becoming a serious health problem. The stench from these mountains of rubbish became quite overpowering in the summer months. UN troops would occasionally come along, pour aviation fuel on them, and set them alight. When not rummaging around refuse, the packs had been known to snap at the elderly and youngsters. Not surprisingly, a number of people received nasty bites. Indeed, some had become victims of savage attacks by the hungry packs of dogs. Bosnian police officers systematically shot them on the spot. A young dog that I had started to feed and train at the warehouse fell victim to police handguns. However, two tiny motherless black Labrador puppies I was looking after and living near the warehouse, (under a broken down crane) were overlooked and continued to survive.

I chose to walk the 1½-miles from the Global Relief Organisation Headquarters to my sleeping accommodation, a hundred or so yards from the front line. As I did not know the back streets very well and wary of getting lost, I ignorantly chose the most dangerous, but direct, route. This took me along the already infamous 'Sniper Alley', adjacent to the front line, which was, as I soon learned, a type of amusement arcade for Serbian snipers. It was dusk, as an adult male of military age, I presented a worthwhile target, and valued as a worthy 'kill'. Considerably more so than the children who were routinely shot in Sarajevo.

I was some thirty yards from safety when an automatic weapon fired a burst from the Serb lines - approximately two hundred yards to my right. Adrenaline took over, I sprinted a further few yards then threw myself onto the ground, tucking in tightly against a three foot high wall offering just about the best protection I was going to get. The burst was very close; no one else was around - I being the only fool that would blatantly expose myself in such a blasé manner, in such a dangerous spot. Even more foolish, and inexcusable; I had already been warned of the danger of Sniper Alley. I distinctly heard the zip of rounds passing nearby, probably fired from a standard Klashnikov AK 47, I thought to myself - not terribly accurate at two hundred yards, but dangerous enough. A single shot from a dedicated sniper's rifle, such as the Russian made Dragunov, based on the AK47, with its powerful telescopic sight would probably not have missed. I lay huddled, hard up against the wall, quickly becoming cold and stiff, as the winter chill swept over my freezing body, daring not to move. I was in control of my senses, but very scared and began to shake with both fear and cold, contemplating how I was going to get out of my self-inflicted predicament. It was important to remain objective and not panic. I looked longingly towards the safety of the Holiday Inn, again thinking; *Is this how I am to die, freezing cold, huddled against a wall, far from home in a strange country, not entirely sure of why I was even there? Hardly the way I imagined my life might end.*

I needed to assess my options. Maybe he thought I had been hit? I hoped so - wouldn't be paying so much attention to my location if that were the case - I thought. At the risk of hypothermia getting the better of me, I decided to wait until complete darkness before zigzagging across the road, to the cover of the concrete pillars supporting the Holiday Inn. From then on, a short distance to one of the many fire escapes that were usually propped open. As the shroud and comfort of darkness arrived, I started to rub some life back into my now stiff legs in preparation for my dash to safety. After a minute or so of this, I got up and ran, willing myself to go faster. Completely exhausted from the short sprint, I made it back safely without coming under fire, having learnt an invaluable lesson.

After this, I decided to stop walking along Sniper Alley, taking my safety more seriously. However, I regularly walked the back streets, believing this to be a safer route to get to work in the morning. The hotel staff, who would look at me as though I was already dead, repeatedly warned me against this. The road was heavily exposed to sniper fire. Indeed, the first three hundred and fifty yards, after leaving the hotel was open ground, with no cover from the prying eyes of the snipers.

In some ignorant macabre way, conveniently forgetting the lesson I had just learned, I saw it as an exciting challenge, every morning, to run these three hundred and fifty yards to the first available cover - then dash across all further open spaces. The build up to the excitement of the dash would start whilst I was having breakfast. The adrenalin rush it gave me would not subside until I had made it safely to the cover of the buildings on the other side of the open ground; having successfully completed my senseless test of 'manhood'. In my favour, I knew it would be difficult to hit a running man with a sniper's rifle and telescopic sights. I knew that the magnified image made it difficult to focus on a fast moving target. Despite this, on a few occasions snipers did shoot at me - hoping for a lucky shot. I knew how stupid it was to make such a defiant gesture, realising that this was all it was. Nevertheless, I did not like being controlled by an enemy I could not see. The lesson I had 'apparently' learned when terrified, snuggled against the wall, and pinned down by a sniper, temporarily forgotten: this being my way of fighting back. I guess it was some kind of youthful defiance.

My morning dance with the Grim Reaper was to come to an abrupt end when, as I neared the Global Relief Organisation Headquarters, an elderly woman was shot dead - three feet in front of me. She was shot in the head, seemingly causing it to explode; throwing her body against an overturned coach, which was serving as an anti-sniping barrier. Her blood spattered against the pale blue rusty roof of the vehicle, as she collapsed lifeless onto the ground. Blood continued to pump momentarily from her head, as she lay motionless. I remember thinking how calm the remainder of her face looked in death - spoilt only by an absurd amount of blood. The majority of the left hand side of her skull having vanished. This time, I was not in an armoured Land Rover and unable to just 'brush off' the incident. After my initial shock, I ran hard and fast, zigzagging for cover, away from the body, pushing aside the fact I could already be in the snipers scope. Others ran in all directions like a startled herd of horses. After finding a suitable place to get my breath and gather my composure, I began to walk, soon arriving at my office.

I was completely anaesthetized by what I had just witnessed and hot and sweaty after my run; I took my coat off. I noticed blood and grey white matter clinging to the blue cloth. Sickened and knowing what it must be, I hurried to the men's room to wash it off. Fortunately, no one else was there, my only company being the dripping tap, echoing throughout, indicating the water supply was on. I caught sight of myself in the mirror above the sink and saw the same deposits of her brain in my hair. Leaning forward, to take a closer look, I saw that it was also on my face and backed away from the mirror in disgust. Repulsed, I was immediately sick, managing to direct the bulk of my half-digested breakfast into the sink; leaving a combination of blood, brains and bile over my head and clothing. What a sight I would look to anyone coming in! With this in mind and determined that no one would see me in this state I hurriedly washed as much of it off as I could, with cold, muddy water. Once cleaned up I walked over to one of the empty toilet cubicles, sat down, and locked the door. The whole occurrence left me confused, not knowing how to handle my feelings. I was too ashamed to talk to anyone and too immature to allow anyone to see me sobbing. I felt guilty and started mumbling,

'Why, oh fucking why?' repeatedly between my increasing tears.

I did not possess the words that could describe how I was feeling on that cold grey morning in Sarajevo. The plain fact was she was dead feeling nothing and I was alive, feeling everything.

Having to once again put a distressing experience behind me, I vowed from then on to use the uncomfortable, top heavy, three and a half ton armoured Land Rover that had been available to me all the time, which, whilst peering through the armoured glass, made the war all the more survivable. I determined the elderly woman's death would not be entirely in vain and would in fact help me stay alive.

Approaching a junction, after leaving our headquarters early, to drive back to my accommodation, I was confronted by a woman lying huddled against a concrete block, serving as an anti-sniping barrier in the middle of the road. A puddle of blood lay around her; she reached an outstretched hand towards me, her eyes pleaded with me to stop. Slowing down, I looked beyond where she lay, towards the Serb lines. Instinctively, I knew there was nothing I could do for her; briefly looking back at her with a stern, calculated, *'you're dead anyway'* expression, dismissing her as a human being, valuing her no more than the concrete block she sheltered behind. To stop and render assistance would have meant my own immediate demise at the hands of the sniper. Therefore, I did not. I had seen it all before on many occasions. The able bodied had gone to the assistance of the wounded and themselves been shot. People who were huddled in nearby cover, waiting their turn to run across the junction, booed and jeered. I calmly drove past, not daring to make eye contact with any of them.

Those wounded by snipers often lay on the ground for hours, slowly bleeding to death, awaiting the final coup-de-grace from a sniper's bullet, ending their misery. I would remain detached and determined not to join them.

I justified my cold, impersonal objective action, by reminding myself that she knew the risk of crossing open junctions and that she should have, and would have known better - it was as simple as that, and anyway, she was just one of the many daily victims - why should I care.

I never regretted my decision not to render assistance; however, once a degree of human empathy returned to me, shortly after arriving home, I remain plagued by the image of her terrified expression, her arm outstretched towards me, pleading for my help - help that I never gave. I now wonder what her last thoughts were, as I coldly decided whilst briefly easing off the accelerator that she was not a viable risk, condemning her to death. Disposable and expendable - not in my remit to assist: drive on.

On a clear bright morning, some days later, whilst driving to work, another elderly woman was hit in the head by a sniper's bullet, some thirty feet in front of my Land Rover. She was lifted bodily, and then fell unceremoniously to the ground - as though some great hand had slammed her body onto the pavement. I instinctively slowed down but once again realised there was nothing I could do for her - she was already dead. Her brain was exposed through the top of her skull; her silvery hair soaked with blood. Her twisted body twitched momentarily in the normal manner briefly after death, then lay perfectly still as blood trickled from her wounds, seeping into her long grey overcoat and onto the pavement. I viewed her as nothing more than a side of freshly culled meat on a butcher's slab - and again drove on. People silently stood cowering in doorways and alleyways nearby, daring not to go near her. It was plain to see there was no point. As I drove slowly past her I scanned the nearby apartment blocks for the sniper; pointlessly guessing the direction and building from which she had been shot. Was anywhere safe? I asked myself. I knew I was, relatively speaking, in my armoured Land Rover. After all that's what really mattered - as far as I was concerned at that moment. Obviously, the sniper thought that this fragile old woman was imperative to the Bosnian war machine, making her a worthy target. Her life came to an abrupt and bloody end a couple of hundred yards or so from the Global Relief Organisation Headquarters, almost under the flag of the Global Relief Organisation, which adorned the building.

Once at work, I stayed in the protection of the Headquarters watching Satellite TV, a re-run of some comedy or another; forgetting that I had just witnessed yet another war crime.

The headquarters was a large modern concrete structure with many offices housing the various Global Relief Organisation departments.

Each department was as equally as important as the other, all 'fighting' their own little office war. Thick communication cables trailed over the floors from the powerful diesel generator on the ground floor, near a little used entrance to the rear of the building. From here the cables climbed the stairs, along passageways and on into the sweltering heat of the radio room: our important and often only reliable link to the outside world.

Boxes containing paper, pens, empty water containers, computers and keyboards, along with printers and fax machines littered the corridors. Outside, concrete slabs surrounded the base of the walls. Large heavy steel plates covered the space where windows had once been. The innocently constructed offices looked more like an ancient fortified hill stronghold, ready to defend itself against a frontal attack from a tribal hoard. Only the oversized Global Relief Organisation flag, and array of aerials and satellite dishes, mounted on the roof, betrayed the true identity of the building. In this case there were no tribal hoards and the enemy in my eyes were the surrounding Serbian infantry, artillery and snipers.

I often looked out of one of the rear facing windows, most of which, although criss - crossed with tape, were still intact (The front windows facing Serbian lines a few hundred yards away were mostly shattered, and far too dangerous to look through). From the relative safety of my vantage point on the second floor, I had an excellent view of a nearby crossroads. I spent considerable time with Karl, a young, highly qualified Swedish water engineer, drinking coffee, watching people scurry, with fearful faces, across the road - hoping not to get shot. A grisly pastime indeed that helped Karl and myself pass many a boring afternoon. It isn't anything I'm proud of; particularly as I had previously witnessed several gruesome killings, right in front of my eyes. Maybe I was becoming ghoulishly indifferent? Perhaps I had seen too much killing in recent times? I'm not sure how I would have felt if I had seen someone killed, during one of my 'voyeuristic' road watching sessions, but fortunately, no one was. This does however, illustrate the depths that I was capable of sinking to. I quite literally could, and am still capable of, detaching myself from death and human suffering - a very useful attribute in war, but completely useless in normal everyday life.

When not at the headquarters, I was either at our warehouse or in the hotel. My accommodation in Sarajevo was cold and spartan. I chose to live in the former Holiday Inn. It was a large hotel, built to western standards and able to withstand mortar and shell fire better than other large buildings in Sarajevo. Most of the worlds press covering this part of the war stayed there. The Holiday Inn must have been one of the ugliest buildings in town. It looked like a concrete block with bizarre bright external yellow tiles. Easy to identify - very easy to hit. However, this unsightly structure proved to be one of the strongest and safest buildings - standing up to frequent direct hits from the shelling.

Many of the Global Relief Organisation personnel lived in flimsy buildings, some in heavily populated and often targeted, predominantly Muslim areas. This, to me, made no sense at all. Despite the grand name, the Holiday Inn was a shadow of its former self. Being so near to the front line, the southern facing wall was pock marked with machine gun fire, anti-aircraft fire and shell fragments. Virtually every window was blown out; many of the rooms were totally uninhabitable. It came to look more and more like an ancient ruin, as every day unplanned changes were added to its structure. As well as smashed windows, panels hung from walls and chunks of masonry regularly disappeared into oblivion whenever the hotel received a direct hit.

One night, as I lay in bed, two explosions followed in quick succession. The Holiday Inn had again been targeted. A rocket passed overhead and exploded behind the building, whilst another blasted the road in front. Debris and shards of razor sharp glass rained out of the sky for a full minute after the impacts. The next day, Martin Bell, a well-known and popular BBC war correspondent whose white jacket became his trademark, broadcast live from the crater. From cover, I watched him film a news report with some trepidation, as he himself was in full view of Serbian snipers.

As time progressed, I didn't even get out of bed when the building received a direct hit - choosing to listen to the volume of mayhem on the corridor outside, to indicate the extent of danger and damage, before making any decision to leave my warm sheets. More often than not, I just turned over and went back to sleep. It is remarkable what you can get used to in time.

The building had been set on fire numerous times by shells tearing open the walls. The Bosnian fire control proved to be very effective, preventing the hotel from burning down, usually whilst I lay fast asleep in bed.

Running up or down the stairs, to get to my room, was quite literally a game of Russian Roulette. The stairway faced the confrontation line and bullets would strike the brickwork, or even come through the large, already broken windows as I made my way to my room. It was always a relief to make it safely. The water supply in the hotel was unpredictable, but electricity was usually available for an hour or two, most days. This would enable me to make a cup of tea, or watch CNN or Sky News - the only channels available on the ancient TV set in my room. Great company all the same. The OJ Simpson trial was under way and the world appeared totally preoccupied with it and gave only moderate coverage of what was happening in Bosnia - unless of course there was sufficient numbers of people killed in a massacre, or similar atrocity to report.

The food supplied in the city's former restaurants and hotels was as unimaginative, as it was bland. Consisting mainly of what I believe was dog or cat food, or even cats and dogs themselves. This was served along with the odd crust of pastry, or if you were lucky some potato soup. It tasted okay, but I found myself living mainly on very poor quality corned beef, donated by the European Economic Community. We often become short of basic provisions, which then necessitated in making do with whatever was available. Even the half-starved local people didn't like to eat the corned beef - so there was nearly always plenty to be had. I supplemented this with army ration packs that I had acquired, which were generally very good. The French rations, were by far the best, similarly followed by the British and German. The accumulated stores of American ration packs were pretty awful, and only eaten as a last resort - or traded with fresh unsuspecting French Foreign Legion troops. Corned beef with dandelion leaves, peas, and tomato sauce was a favourite concoction of mine for some time - all cooked on a small army hexi-block burner; strictly forbidden in the hotel rules - quite ironic really, since the hotel was so often set on fire by shelling.

Breakfast, provided by the hotel was a little better. Served underground, for obvious safety reasons, in what was previously the hotel disco. Boiled eggs, fried eggs or omelette and bread - there was little else to eat and sometimes nothing at all. The one thousand two hundred Deutchemarks, roughly eight hundred dollars per week, it cost the Global Relief Organisation for me to stay was paid irrespective of whether there was electricity, water or even food. Presumably, a portion of this was used to buy weapons and ammunition - in support of the Bosnian Muslim war effort.

The Global Relief Organisation Finance Administrator did his best to persuade me to move out of the hotel because of the expense. I vehemently refused on security grounds, stubbornly telling him to make his savings elsewhere. I was comfortable on the seventh floor with several floors above me, acting as a sponge throughout the conflict, soaking up many incoming shells. It was considerably cheaper to stay on the top floors of the hotel, but they were, for obvious reasons, seldom occupied.

Firefights outside the Holiday Inn and across the confrontation line regularly took place. Both Serbian and Muslim gunners raked nearby buildings with heavy machine gun fire in an effort to flush out and kill snipers. The top floors of the Holiday Inn were often directly targeted: leading me to believe BiH snipers were taking advantage of this high building; hoping the presence of neutral international staff would prohibit the possibility of return fire. It did not. Serbian snipers despised the presence of international representatives, almost as much as the Bosnian Muslim snipers they were trying to kill - and cared little for international casualties, either aid workers or press.

I awoke one Sunday morning to a deafening crescendo of multiple machine gun and anti-aircraft fire, used in a ground support role, immediately outside my window. Instinctively, I slid onto the floor donning my bullet-proof vest and helmet that were always on hand, before cautiously stealing a wary glance through my window. I could see a French AMX 10 armoured vehicle, calmly traversing its powerful 105mm gun towards Serbian lines, hunting for a target. Fighting was taking place to the front of the Holiday Inn. I slowly made my way crawling under windows to gain access to one of the south facing rooms - to assess the situation. I believed, due to the volume and close proximity of fire, that this was a major Serbian offensive. As we were so close to the front line, we were in danger of being overrun - my worst fear. Would they kill the international staff in the Holiday Inn in an unstoppable orgy of killing? Then make some sort of diplomatic apology, saying they were unable to identify neutral international staff from Bosnian combatants. Nothing would surprise me.

Again, I had that feeling of wanting to fire back. Not since Gorni Vakuf - nearly two years before - had I felt this way. This time to defend my new, albeit, temporary home. I had to remind myself that my mission was one of peace and questioned why I was feeling this way.

I steered my thoughts back to my current options. Should I make my way to the comparative safety of the warehouse and my armoured truck? That would mean having to make the exposed dash outside the Holiday Inn. Pretty dangerous with so much shooting going on. Alternatively, I could stay put like a sitting duck ready to take flight - should my worst fear come to fruition.

In actual fact, the French Legionnaires and Serbs were in a fierce battle to gain control of a bridge over the River Sava, running parallel to the Holiday Inn. The bridge served as one of many dividing lines between Serbian and Muslim communities. The day before, the Serbs had taken control of the bridge by force, from the lightly armed French soldiers, killing one of them in the process. The French had issued the Serbs with an ultimatum, which, as expected, was ignored. They were in the process of recapturing their sand bagged positions near the bridge entrance. Thus enabling them to recover the tactical advantage, and no less important to them, restoring their now damaged credibility. In the battle, lasting several hours, two more French, and two Serb' soldiers were killed. An additional Serb' was captured before the French regained control - in this early morning raid. The rest of the day was calm and typically uneventful. In fact, I remember watching the Formula One Grand Prix on television that afternoon, feeling quite pleased that the French had managed to maintain the status quo and restore a buffer zone between myself and Serbian lines.

Some evenings when it was quiet and there was food, I would occasionally go out with colleagues to one of the struggling local restaurants still trading in Sarajevo. I derived no pleasure from sitting in an exposed eating house, situated on the side of a gentle hill, not knowing what I was eating or if a shell would, or wouldn't, destroy us. On many occasions, I would sit with Hans, my friend, half-listening to him speaking in his native language, whilst my thoughts and vision were focused towards the front line. I hoped no shells would come our way and never sat by windows - as many had bullet holes. This legacy remains with me to this day.

A locally employed supervisor, two local truck drivers and two elderly warehousemen staffed our warehouse storing food, medicines, and water sanitation equipment. The local drivers were not issued with flak-jackets or helmets. I felt this was grossly unfair on the part of the Global Relief Organisation Management. Although they did not cross confrontation lines, they risked their lives on a daily basis, carrying out their duties facing the same hazards as I from shelling and sniping. It was as though my life was worth more than theirs and they weren't worthy of protection. I felt that this was unjust and approached the Global Relief Organisation who responded by saying,

'They would probably only sell them anyway' I did not accept this and continued to raise the matter strongly at our regular security briefings. My dogged persistence was not in vain, and ultimately they were issued with protective equipment. This helped the local staff bond with us, and boosted their morale. We considered ourselves lucky that the city authorities allowed us any staff at all, as most able-bodied men were serving on the front line, or engaged in other duties supporting their troops. The least we could do was look after them. Even old people had to spend odd weeks filling sandbags and cooking for soldiers on the front line and if our workers were killed, it was unlikely that we would get replacements. Therefore, it was in our interest to try to keep them alive.

The two drivers who kept the local hospitals supplied with medicines and food, also acted as 'taxi' drivers for Global Relief Organisation Staff. Neither of them could leave the city even to visit local suburbs. Their Global Relief Organisation status would not have guaranteed their return. If detained, they would have been lucky to be made prisoners of war, more probably, they would have been taken to the side of the road and shot - such was the hatred between the divided communities.

Like other relief organisations, the Global Relief Organisation endeavoured to help all victims of war based on their needs. The kitchens that had been set up in the nearby Serb' suburbs required a delivery of food, medicines and water purification tablets once per week - or whenever we had supplies to distribute. The Serb' population in their own village-sized enclaves were just as hungry as the besieged Bosnian Muslim population that lived near by. The one daily wholesome meal provided by the Global Relief Organisation for some adults and children, helped keep starvation at bay - but only just. Powdered milk was provided for babies and the very young. The kitchens throughout Sarajevo and suburbs were a resounding success, but were only available to the most vulnerable of citizens. This was usually the very old or very young.

To my knowledge, the Serbian population was largely ignorant to the fact that the relief flights into Sarajevo Airport and incoming truck convoys, included supplies for the Serbian population too. After attacks on the airport and relief aircraft, the airport would often be shut down - sometimes for weeks on end. During spells of closure, negotiation between UN and senior Serbian officials would take place. No doubt, UN representatives would highlight the neutrality of the United Nations, and all other aid organisations, in a vain effort to ensure the Serbs would not 'disrupt the activities of the relief effort'.

Incoming flights were disrupted for the whole duration of my stay. Despite guarantees given by the Serbs not to shoot at relief aircraft, landing at Sarajevo Airport was always a precarious affair. On one occasion after flying out of Sarajevo, and landing at Zagreb in Croatia, four heavy machine gun holes were identified in the tail section of the French Lockheed C130 Hercules transport that I had disembarked from. Not enough to do any significant damage to an aircraft as large as a C130, but disconcerting all the same.

Whenever relief aircraft were attacked, no supplies entered Sarajevo. Serbs in the surrounding suburbs and villages would be just as hungry as the Bosnian Muslims within the city itself. Such is the utter stupidity of war and periodic defiance showed by all to the UN.

The local drivers had previously assisted the two old warehousemen in digging a shelter in the railway embankment, opposite the warehouse. This shelter was well made and very safe, with steps carved out of the earth leading up to it. The entrance was heavily sandbagged and formed an L shape, preventing any shrapnel from entering directly through the entrance. It served us well, although it probably would not protect its occupants from a direct hit from a high explosive shell.

Despite all their hard work in constructing the shelter, on one occasion, during heavy shelling, I noticed the two old warehousemen, crouched in a foetal position, pressed hard against the warehouse wall. The impacts were very close, almost on top of us in fact. They dared not make the thirty-foot dash across the courtyard to the shelter, somewhat undermining their efforts in making it in the first place. It was far more dangerous to stay put in the warehouse - as it had only a thin corrugated roof. One direct hit would have finished us all.

Regardless of the dangers in the city, and despite the problems in getting the local drivers' body armour, every effort was made to look after locally employed staff, both at the warehouse and Headquarters. They all worked very hard and were extremely loyal, regardless of the appalling conditions, constant fear, and meagre diet.

Hans and I often visited different suburbs of Sarajevo to assess the warehousing and security arrangements, prior to, and with a view to, making regular deliveries. It was also important for us to establish that there would be enough able-bodied men to unload the trucks. Although there were forklift trucks, most had long since broken down, with no spares being available. Rarely was there diesel for the forklift trucks that remained serviceable: unloading was mostly done by hand. Five thousand individual family parcels containing items such as flour, sugar, rice, tins of corned beef and soap, could take considerable time to unload with only a couple of men and prolonged our exposure - making us vulnerable to attack. Sacks of rice, flour and beans could take even longer, so it was important to make a thorough risk assessment, prior to the arrival of a fully laden truck. Even the geographical position of a given location had to be taken into account - if exposed to a nearby front line.

Sometimes, in gratitude for a delivery of aid, whole villages of malnourished residents would emerge from their homes forming a human chain from the truck to wherever the supplies were to be stored. At this point, I would quite happily supervise them unloading!

One afternoon, when returning from such a venture with Hans, we took a wrong turning. This was easily done, there being no road signs in 'No-Mans-Land' (the unoccupied territory separating opposing forces) and few features that would be recognisable on our inaccurate maps. We ended up amongst the rubble of what was once a village, some four miles north of the Serbian held town of Rajlavac, its inhabitants dead or displaced long ago. The town had been fought over many times; no building was left undamaged. In fact, most had only the odd wall left standing - scarred by shrapnel and bullets. The town resembled another Balkan Stalingrad, bereft of any living human presence. It was hard to believe that these very roads were once alive with people chatting, children playing, shops, and traffic.

We proceeded slowly and with caution, taking particular note of any unusual looking bumps in the road, ensuring that we drove on well defined tyre or preferably armoured track marks (less likely to be falsely laid) to minimise the risk of driving over a mine. The devastation made it difficult to define where the road actually was. I strained my eyes looking for trip wires stretched just above the road that might detonate a concealed claymore-mine, hidden in the rubble or undergrowth: undergrowth that Mother Nature was claiming back, rightly believing it was hers. There were many of these devices left over from recent battles. They were positioned on roadsides or paths to ambush or alert an opposing force of an enemy's presence. One of these mines, if detonated, would send several hundred ball bearings at high velocity into the side of the Land Rover, mutilating the occupants. Unexploded mortars also littered the area. Human debris scattered the village landscape in a backdrop of seemingly hopeless, unnecessary destruction.

Both Hans and I stared in horror at bodily remains of men killed during recent fighting, slumped over walls, randomly scattered on the road or heaped in small clusters: their hands tied behind their backs seemingly captured and executed on the side of the road. Tattered blood stained uniforms covered their rotting bodies in various states of decomposition. Most in fact were now skeletons, some still wearing the standard Yugoslavian issue helmet, strapped neatly to their whitish smiling skulls: staring, emptily at us, the new intruders, daring to disturb their peace. I felt pulled into their now calm world of serenity. Other, less decayed corpses had whispers of hair on their scalps and patches of blackened skin visible through their blood stained camouflaged - torn uniforms. Maggots and flies long having finished their trade... It was frighteningly eerie. The silence made me feel nervous and uncomfortable. We had to get out of this 'opencast' graveyard and leave these poor souls to rest.

Neither of us wanted to go back through the village, and in the knowledge that we were heading in a south-easterly direction towards Sarajevo we discussed our options. We decided to continue along the same route. There were no recognisable landmarks making it very difficult to distinguish road junctions. It was important we pressed on. We had a limited time, granted by Serb' authorities to remain in their territory. They would have been only too willing to arrest us as spies, for loitering in an area that we had no authority to be in.

This fear was totally justified and resulted from an American Convoy Leader and five French drivers who, like us, had strayed into 'forbidden' territory. They were currently languishing in nearby Lukovica barracks held by the Serbs. Lukovica Barracks was the headquarters and forward base, being less than a mile from the front line, of the Serbian Romanija Corps - commanded by the reputedly ruthless General Galić. The barracks was often used for meeting UN representatives, to discuss the many, none functioning ceasefire arrangements. The imprisoned convoy drivers were charged with 'Supplying the BiH with equipment that could facilitate war.' A trumped up charge if I have ever heard of one!

Several weeks' later, we heard that their aid organisation had paid an undisclosed sum for their release on bail (the rumour was around sixty thousand Deutchemarks), pending appearance at the Republika of Srbska Peoples court. Of course, once returned to their organisation, they were swiftly flown out of Sarajevo; the aid organisation forfeiting the 'ransom', happy to have its members safely returned. The Serb' authorities, knowing full well that they would be evacuated, similarly happy to retain the sixty thousand Deutchemarks bail money, to further their own increasingly cash stricken war effort.

Chapter Seven

Those with money fled to Italy, Austria and Germany, as the Serbian noose closed around the city. Many had no alternative but to stay. A few were more privileged, having a second chance to escape.

In early March 1995, Zorren, the warehouse supervisor with whom I had become good friends, received notification that he was to rejoin a front line infantry unit - defending the trenches on the outskirts of the city. At the outbreak of war, his wife and child escaped to Italy to stay with friends. Zorren chose to stay behind to look after their house. However, he had already served six months on the front line, receiving a bullet wound to his right leg. He was now rightfully fearful of going back to the trenches having one week's notice to prepare. In the short time we had available, we devised a daring plan that would re-unite him with his wife and daughter. It was going to be risky - for both of us, but with forethought and planning I was confident that we could pull it off.

The entrance to the airport at Sarajevo was heavily guarded; firstly by a Bosnian Army Checkpoint, and a little further on, a French Army Checkpoint. As planned, over the next six days and during my regular trips to the airport, I nurtured my business-like friendship with the Bosnian guards, making mental notes of the most amicable, and those most likely to search the vehicle. I would often sit with them and drink Slivovitz, a locally produced nauseous spirit, in an effort to gain their trust: purposely leaving the Land Rover's door ajar. I hoped this furthered the subconscious impression that I was an open person who could be trusted and had nothing to hide. The French usually only took the vehicle's registration number, checked my identification card, and waved me through: this was soon to change.

The plan was to smuggle Zorren onto an aid flight out of Sarajevo, bound for Italy. I anticipated any attempt would be particularly difficult and fraught with danger. The security at French Checkpoints had recently been tightened, almost to a state of paranoia: Serbian soldiers, dressed in French Army uniform, had been driving around the city in light armoured personnel carriers, previously stolen from the French at gunpoint - earlier on in the war. They would make regular detailed reconnaissance trips around the city. Like all French military vehicles, the Serb' impostors were casually waved through all French Checkpoints. Consequently, everyone's identification was now thoroughly checked and vehicles inspected as they traversed in and out of the city and, in particular, the entrance to the airport. Despite this, we decided to proceed as planned. I hoped the French knew me well enough by now not to warrant a thorough search. It was nonetheless going to be risky.

On March 7[th,] at around 1.30 pm I met Zorren at the warehouse. If all went well the Bosnian guards at the airport would be dozing after their lunch, and not be too interested in doing anything other than giving me a complementary wave as I passed through. We had rehearsed what we were to do if Zorren was discovered. I was to plead total ignorance and express shock and anger at him being found in my vehicle, going as far as pushing him forcefully towards the guards, in an attempt to disassociate myself with this escapee.

On the day of his planned escape, I had asked Zorren to pack only a small holdall, so as not to arouse suspicion, should anyone see him getting into the Land Rover. Zorren climbed aboard, curled up, and covered himself with a blanket. He looked terrified as I threw another blanket and a couple of towropes over him. Much to his groaning displeasure, I lodged a heavy spare Land Rover wheel on top of him.

That should suffice, and wasn't untypical of how my Land Rover would normally look - I thought to myself. I was feeling confident and without anxiety, hoping Zorren's nerve would hold.

I drove to the first checkpoint, stopped and said in my normal friendly manner, 'Dobra jutra, Kako ste?' ('Good morning, how are you?'). Despite it being the afternoon, they always appreciated my efforts to speak in their language.

'Dobra, dobra, hvuala' ('Good, good, thank you') - the soldier replied. He recognised me and trusted me as a friend; took the vehicle registration number, quickly glanced in the back of the Land Rover and waved me through. The 'friendship' I had nurtured paid off. I breathed a small sigh of relief, remaining totally composed, preparing myself for what I anticipated to be the more difficult French Checkpoint.

At the French Checkpoint I said nothing more than 'Bonjour' (the French were always business like and trying to engage in conversation would have served no useful purpose - so I didn't). I handed my identification through the already opened side window. It was checked thoroughly. I sat looking out towards the airport as the soldier went to the back of my vehicle. I hoped he wouldn't open the door - which wasn't locked. He recorded the Belgian registration number, came back to side window and waved me through. Easy!

We had both just taken an incredible risk. Zorren and I, if caught, would have been arrested and instantly detained. The consequences of detention were somewhat worse for Zorren. He could have quite easily been imprisoned for desertion if captured and handed over to his countrymen. The worst that could happen to me in the long term, would be a few days imprisonment, interrogation and a dishonourable deportation - which I had prepared myself for in the event of it all going wrong. Our mission had gone well, but wasn't yet over. An aid flight was due in shortly but could be turned back if fighting broke out near to the airport.

Military staff had priority on outgoing flights, followed by aid organisations and then members of the press. Therefore, until Zorren was on the flight, there was no guarantee that I wouldn't have to smuggle him back into the city. The whole process to be repeated once again. Time, for Zorren at least, was running out.

After stopping near the departure terminal, I opened the rear door of the Land Rover and called Zorren. He got out, knelt on the floor with his head in his hands (this seemed to be a peculiar trait of the Bosnians). His behaviour worried me; this would draw attention to us as security inside the airport was quite intense. Meanwhile I saw Zorren's aeroplane approaching the runway on final approach. I was trying to act in a normal, casual manner, not wanting us to look any different than on any other visit to the airport. He looked very pale,

'I lost ten years of my life at both of those checkpoints,' he said.

'Come on, you're not out yet, but yer planes here', I replied in acknowledgement, whilst helping him to his feet. I was feeling much the same myself but quite confidant that the escape plan was going to work. Zorren stood up, turned to the Land Rover and retrieved his small bag. He then thanked me for my help in a typical Bosnian over demonstrative bear hug - usually reserved for family members.

'For fucks sake just go Zorren, get on that bloody plane and get the fuck out while you can.' I faced him, gripping his shoulders, looked him in the eye, and told him *not* to look back. I could sense some of the pain and uncertainty he was feeling. I saw him take out his Global Relief Organisation Identity Card from inside his jacket as he made his way to Departures. He didn't look back.

For my part, I returned through both checkpoints with surprising ease. The Bosnian guards again recognised me as their friend, which I was, and quite simply gestured me through. I waved back, again breathing a sigh of relief.

An hour later, the French Lockheed C130 Hercules took off, presumably heading for the airport in Ancona, Italy. At least that was where I hoped it was going. Zorren had escaped and all being well would soon be with his wife and daughter. Two weeks' later, as agreed, he sent a card via the Global Relief Organisation, addressed to all the staff in Sarajevo. He said that all was well and that he was now with his family staying with friends somewhere in Italy. I paid little notice, not wanting to draw any attention but discreetly smiled to myself feeling quite proud. I, along with others, wondered how he, and many others in Sarajevo working for the various organisations were managing to escape.

I thought this was the last I would hear of Zorren, but two weeks' after the successful escape, Bosnian police came looking for him at the warehouse. Two plain-clothed officers identified themselves to me in their stumbling English, wanting to question me on his whereabouts...

They interviewed me in my tiny candle lit office, tucked away in the corner of the warehouse. I sat one side of the plain wooden table and they the other. I asked one of the warehouse staff to make some coffee; specifically requesting the Turkish variety that I hated but knew the Bosnian police would warm to. They probably hadn't seen anything like the quality of coffee that I had obtained from the Black Market for quite some time. Maybe they had their own ill-gotten supplies. It had proved a good bargaining tool and pacifier in the past and was usually difficult to obtain in Bosnia. I hoped my kind offering would help them 'bond' with me.

'I know nothing and would never aid an escape; more than my job's worth, completely against my own and Global Relief Organisation principles. Look, I need all the staff we can get here, you're wasting you're time. Do you *honestly* think I would do such a thing?'

They weren't fools and strongly suspected that he had left the country knowing that I was in a position to help. I began to think they knew more about the incident than they were letting on, but remained self-assured and calm. I was told quite bluntly that if I didn't cooperate that I would be arrested. The coffee bonding obviously wasn't working.

'I am cooperating,' I hastened to add, 'Doing everything I can to help. I've told you, I don't want to lose any more staff.'

To help someone avoid military service, or even worse, escape the city, was a very serious offence. No one was allowed to leave. The Bosnian authorities strictly forbade it. The police officers said the finger of suspicion was firmly pointed at me after making enquiries about Zorren's whereabouts. They weren't going to let on what enquiries these were, but I remained silent and confident not asking too many questions. After forty-five minutes or so, they left. I had work to do. The expression on their faces indicated that they weren't convinced. I hadn't told anyone of our escape plans and didn't suspect Zorren would have told anyone either. I knew the police would be back and had to seriously think about my predicament. I wasn't sure if they were bluffing or not.

I wasn't going to lose sleep over it, after all I had diplomatic status in Bosnia. Surely, they wouldn't want the embarrassment of arresting me. I thought about it for the next couple of days but felt confident that the whole affair would not go any further. The locally employed staff at the Global Relief Organisation warehouse in Sarajevo knew Zorren and I had been good friends. Had any of them overheard us planning the escape? Had the police interviewed any of them before me, making veiled threats to them, to spill the beans - so to speak? After all this was previously a communist led country and such occurrences were certainly not unheard of, almost a way of life and a legacy of the former 'police state' regime? Had someone at the airport seen me with Zorren as I encouraged him to get up, when he was kneeling on the ground with his head buried in his hands? Indeed, had they visited the airport and checked who was on each flight for the last two weeks? Had they seen Zorren's name and my vehicle at the airport on the same day? I didn't know and without raising suspicion had no way of finding out.

After thinking long and hard I felt that the police weren't just fishing for information, and from their confident tone, I deduced that they did in fact know more than they were letting on. I was convinced they were gathering enough evidence to arrest me, with a view to deportation - or remove me from the equation altogether - in a quicker more effective manner. Unlikely, but anything can, and does happen in war, and I knew the Bosnian authorities were desperate to avoid the city being drained of any more able-bodied men. Thousands had escaped before the Serbian Army encircled the city and they weren't going to allow the loss of any more valuable human resources.

Unorthodox measures were needed: I decided to visit the Bosnian Police Commander at his Headquarters in Sarajevo. This could indeed backfire (and result in my detention). I was sufficiently confident in my negotiating and reasoning skills, and under the circumstances, believed I could avoid the investigation going any further.

Sugar Coated War

The purpose of the visit was to stop any further enquiries being made into Zorren's whereabouts. What was known was known and what was not known should remain that way. Before doing so, I chose to confide the whole story to Alma - the secretary who worked for us, who, being local would act as my translator. She listened intently and was pleased to help.

It was not difficult for us to gain access past the guards at the entrance to the headquarters, explaining that I needed to see their commander. My passport and identification card carried some weight with the Bosnian authorities. They were always keen to welcome any contact with the Global Relief Organisation. After all, we had done a considerable amount to ease the suffering of the people of Sarajevo and no doubt some of our supplies destined for the suffering innocent, ended up with the police.

After explaining who I was, he said he was aware of the 'investigation' that I was referring to. He ordered coffee - it was good. (I wasn't after all the only person to have quality coffee In Sarajevo). Maybe the police who visited me at the warehouse weren't so impressed after all. I indicated to him that we should talk about the 'unfortunate' disappearance of Zorren. Despite my self-belief, and in the knowledge that I had diplomatic protection, the Commander quickly understood the true purpose of my visit. He was, in true corrupt communist style, willing to negotiate and do 'business'.

In exchange for the investigation into Zorren's whereabouts being dropped, and with me of course admitting nothing, I arranged for a 'few' bags of sugar, flour and blankets to be delivered to the Bosnian Police Headquarters the following day; for them to distribute amongst themselves as they saw fit - no questions asked. It saved embarrassment for all concerned and kept me from being deported and bringing the Global Relief Organisation into disrepute. The integrity of the Global Relief Organisation remained intact and I remained free. I believed this was a small price to pay for Zorren's freedom and the fat middle aged Commander no doubt equally saw it as fair!

Neither Zorren nor his family would ever be able to return to Bosnia. Despite his previous brave labours, he is now branded a deserter. The Global Relief Organisation was completely unaware of my efforts in helping Zorren to escape, and would never have condoned my actions. This would have compromised the organisation's impartiality towards any one side in the war. In essence, it was wrong of me to engage in such activities, as there was more at stake than I realised at the time. However, by now, I felt that I was fighting my own small war. By helping Zorren gain his freedom, I had just won a small victory, albeit at a dangerous price.

A local man named Vojo took Zorren's job at the warehouse. He was a Serb', living in ethnically mixed Sarajevo. Prior to the outbreak of war, Vojo worked in a research laboratory of a company manufacturing telescopic sights, some of which were now being used by his fellow Serbs to target people in the city, Serbs included. Attacking Serb' forces considered Vojo and others like him, as traitors, since they had chosen to stay in their homes rather than fight for the Serbian cause. He was expected to leave for Greater Serbia and along with his family, become impoverished nomadic refugees. I spent many hours with Vojo during shelling, sitting in the shelter discussing the war and life before the war under Tito; it fascinated me. We also compared life in the West and the similarities between our upbringing and cultures.

Vojo was indeed a man of intellect. His command of the English language was such that we were able to converse in deep conversation, discussing whether the war was in fact a civil war as the West liked to presume, or in fact a war of independence in the accepted sense. Vojo was adamant it was a war of independence whilst I saw it as a civil war. We did however agree that, as was the case in most conflicts since World War II, that this war was utterly senseless. As shells poured into the city around us, and the explosions reverberated throughout the warehouse, I often noticed Vojo's mind straying from our discussion. He always remained aware that his wife and young daughter could easily be the next victims of the Serbian artillery. For him and his family this was a war of survival; for me it was a war of choice - and something of an adventure. We never discussed the future. No one in Sarajevo believed there was one.

In the evenings, after work, I would find a vantage point at the top of the hotel where, with a warm coffee and some army oatmeal biscuits, I would sit back and observe the nightly ritual firefight across

Sarajevo. Initially, I found it quite fascinating, listening to explosions and watching tracer rounds of differing colours flashing across the unlit sky. The noise of nearby impacting shells made the whole building shake, sometimes causing me to crouch, spilling my valuable coffee. These shows were the most captivating but nevertheless deadly, and most violent fireworks displays that I witnessed throughout the whole of the war.

However, the novelty eventually wore off and the spectacle of light and noise made me realise how hopeless the situation was quickly becoming for the people of Sarajevo. So much for us to do - and so little seemingly possible. Every bullet or impacting mortar round quite possibly meant the end of someone's life - or a home destroyed. The adrenalin rush that I felt at the time of Zorren's escape had long since subsided. I became reclusive and spent more time listening to the BBC World Service on my small, battery-powered radio, lying on my bed trying to make sense of it all. The near constant sound of incoming and outgoing shells became nothing more than part of everyday life.

At weekends, I often entered my room on Friday and not leave until going to work on Monday morning - apart from the odd excursion to the warehouse to check it hadn't been demolished; and that the valuable vehicles were intact. This, of course, depended upon how safe it was to drive at any given time. I had long given up walking the streets of Sarajevo and going to the market or just looking around the old part of the city. It was quite simply too dangerous and far safer to stay in my room with my personal radio on standby, so that if necessary I could be contacted.

To help combat loneliness, I acquired books from weekly visits to the British Embassy, which accommodated a very well stocked library in a room with posters of London and stereotypical quaint English villages. I immediately felt at home with the 'Britishness' and very relaxed in this environment, re-acquiring my identity as an Englishman and making a couple of new friends too. The library was open to all British Nationals working in the city, much to the envy of other foreign personnel, who's embassies did not offer such a service to their own people. A legacy of Britain's colonial past? Tea and coffee, along with fairly recent newspapers and magazines, were usually available. More importantly was the fact that there were people who spoke English as a first language, enabling me to speak naturally, not in a slow, over compensating manner that I was now accustomed to.

The ambassador's wife was clearly an educated woman, with whom I enjoyed conversation. She would tell me about life in the diplomatic service, and the shrinking opportunities now available for overseas service with the Foreign Office. There must be many other postings that would not have subjected her and her husband to the brutalities of this war. Like myself, she was not compelled to be there but chose to support her husband, in his role as ambassador preserving British interests in this part of the world. The embassy was situated in a Muslim part of the city, which was often subjected to particularly heavy shelling, but up until now had not been hit.

I began to spend as much time at the embassy as I could, borrowing many books, spending many hours in my hotel room; sharing time between reading by candlelight and listening to the radio: as the city and its inhabitants were slowly torn apart by shells.

There was a satellite telephone located in the headquarters. It was incredibly expensive to use, and the Global Relief Organisation, unlike the United Nations did not give us any free usage. Nevertheless, there was a landline out of Sarajevo and for a small fee I was able to telephone friends and family at home. It was wonderful to talk with people at home. The route the line took out of Sarajevo was a closely guarded secret, but I expect it ran under the recently dug tunnel underneath Sarajevo Airport and through into friendly territory. The line was known to be 'bugged' and caution was always exercised when speaking. On several occasions, I was cut off mid-sentence. This always seemed to happen when whoever I was talking to spoke of politics or asked anything of a military nature. In a rather childish manner, I used to taunt the 'listeners', to let them know I knew that my conversation was being monitored. However, by prior arrangement, my local hometown BBC Radio station telephoned me at the HQ and I gave an interview describing recent events. This, to my amazement, was not terminated prematurely and was broadcast live.

During the summer, Martin Bell, reporting for the BBC and his crew returned to Sarajevo. They usually spent two weeks in the city and two weeks out - travel permitting.

I looked forward to them being there, as they always made me particularly welcome and although I normally did not drink, I gladly accepted their hospitality. It was great to be amongst Brits!

The BBC team would set up their camera facing southwards, overlooking the nearby Old Jewish Cemetery, which was 'No-Mans-Land' and constantly fought over. Even the dead weren't safe, as shells impacted upon their graves. During attacks, the freshly killed would fall upon the dead of another era.

I would happily gossip the night away with the crew whilst their camera recorded some of the most bitter combat footage of the war. I felt that Martin, now retired from the BBC, had a very calming influence on those around him and his quiet composed manner was one that, unknown to him, I enjoyed and came to respect. His coverage of the war was as diverse as it was thorough. His experience of covering conflicts was clearly evident through the quality of his work.

Other TV networks from all over the world descended upon Sarajevo, by now often described as the most dangerous place on earth, something that I, in my early days in the city, didn't really comprehend or understand. However, by the time I left, I wholly agreed with , fully understanding the description. Central News Network (CNN) and other American news agencies provided rapid up-to-date coverage, as did Sky News from the United Kingdom, RTL from Germany, and a few other European media corporations. On occasion, when I had access to a TV and the war was broadcast live, I watched the events on TV as they literally unfolded outside my hotel room. This was quite an uncanny phenomenon, as most people would be watching the same pictures from the safety of their living rooms - thousands of miles away.

American Broadcasting Company (ABC) was a network of particular interest to me. Not necessarily for its media presentation skills, or quality of work, which I'm sure was good, but because whenever the crew came to stay in the Holiday Inn, they would bring vast amounts of beer, spirits and buffet type food in a typically overburdened, over the top, American style. I never understood how the team managed it, and presumed that they were veterans of many conflicts and knew far more about bribery and smuggling than I did. All foreign nationals working in Sarajevo, together with journalists and press, living in the Holiday Inn were invited to their 'press social evenings', where the food was laid out for all to enjoy. I felt for the hotel staff looking on in their ill-fitting uniforms - due to weight loss. Under hotel rules they were forbidden from having any of the food. I expect they thought of it as just another example of western decadence. American generosity knew no bounds and neither did my greed at this occasional, unexpected treat!

Even the normally aloof Global Relief Organisation Personnel attended and seemed to enjoy themselves. After four cans of lager, I summed up enough courage to chat to a young attractive Belgian delegate, whom every male in the headquarters was trying to get into bed: me included. I really thought my luck was in, as she initially seemed to respond positively to my dishonourable advances. It turned out that Eve was not impressed with my alcohol inspired confidence, despite me trying to convince her I wasn't drunk. She said, in her innocence, that I should go to bed, as I was drunk. At that point, she led me from the party to my room. Yes! I thought. She's definitely up for it. 'Wait 'till I tell Karl about this'. I thought to myself.

A couple of minutes down the corridor we arrived at my hotel room door. I fumbled for the key - she led me in.

'This is gonna be fuckin' great.' I thought.

'First shag in how many months?'

I lay back pulling her on top of me whilst trying to kiss her neck and strategically placing my hand under her loose fitting tea shirt, in an attempt to get her bra off. All I'm afraid to say rather clumsily. The alcohol was really taking effect.

Eve sprang to her feet, as though someone had passed a high voltage current through her body. She slapped me so hard across my face that I momentarily saw stars - then told me I was a filthy English pig, or something similar in French. She then made hastily for the door - whilst straightening her twisted bra strap. What have I done wrong? I foolishly asked myself whilst rubbing my cheek. I'm sure she was up for it.

'Cock teasing bitch' I shouted after her as I turned over and went to sleep. She was nevertheless right - I was behaving like a filthy pig.

Chapter Eight

Occasionally in war, there are dangerous, but comical occurrences, which bring a morbid black humour to those who work amongst death on a daily basis.

One Friday morning, after delivering flour to a local bakery, (where I had to pay for my bread despite me delivering the flour free of charge!), and driving back to Headquarters, I noticed a man sitting with the driver's door of his car open. His legs stretched out in front of him onto the ground. Paying closer attention, I further noticed parts of the road next to his feet erupting into the air. Easing off the throttle, I watched as the man looked down at the road, utterly mystified at what was happening. All of a sudden, he realised that he was been shot at by a sniper, and threw himself across the seats of his car. I chuckled to myself, sitting with relative impunity in my armoured truck. It was like a sketch from an old classic Monty Python film. Laughing, I momentarily forgot that this man's life had just been seriously compromised. Was I becoming indifferent to other people's suffering, cocooned in the safety of my Kevlar cab? At that moment, quite positively, yes.

Occasionally, I would play football with some of the local lads. I'm not a football enthusiast, but felt it was always good, where possible to build up a rapport with locally employed staff. We would play in an abandoned warehouse, centrally located in the city: quite often shelling would start. The game would freeze temporarily as incoming shells could be heard overhead, with everyone looking up at the ceiling. Then, when the detonation occurred, a short distance away, the game continued as, for that moment the danger had passed us by. This made me extremely nervous and completely ruined my already limited ability to play the game. The momentary pause would give me some respite from the repeated bruising blows of the ball. I was useless and felt that the Bosnian players gained considerable pleasure from using me as the footballers' equivalent of a punch bag!

Mid May 1995 was hot. There was an air of misplaced optimism that a recently locally agreed ceasefire would be resumed, and that the frantic sniping that both sides had perpetrated over the previous few days would cease. This would allow the movement of supplies to take place more freely around the city without the constant fear of being shot. It would also give the inhabitants a semblance of normality - at least until one side or the other decided it was over, whereupon the killing and fear of being killed would resume.

Our radio operator at the Headquarters, Goran, a Sarajevan Muslim, was to marry his long time fiancée Tanja. I had an invitation to his wedding, which was soon to take place. I didn't know him very well, but was familiar with his voice over the radio, and anyway weddings meant I could gorge on whatever food was available. I was yet to meet his future wife and quite looked forward to a break in the dismal monotony, that now prevailed in the besieged city, and of course any extra provisions that may be available.

The service was simple and held in a nearby severely damaged mosque, which was amazingly still standing after numerous direct hits. I remember going into the mosque, not being too sure whether this was an entirely wise thing to do. Not only were mosques a favourite target for bored Serbian artillerymen located in the surrounding hills; a large gathering of people providing an added bonus, even more so if a Muslim wedding was in process. The Serbs had no reservations about shelling funeral gatherings so I didn't anticipate there being any issues of morality in shelling wedding ceremonies. The building itself looked as though it was already just about to fall down. One more direct hit and I'm sure it would have done. Fortunately, the ceremony was short and passed off without incident. The bride and groom, in a misplaced heaven after getting wed, made their way to a nearby café that had been hired for the reception, closely followed by a very nervous entourage. In my typically cynical manner that prevailed at the time, I reasoned that if they were to be killed on their wedding day, (which was still possible) that it would surely be one of the shortest marriages in history. They would die together having never split up. Isn't that what most newly weds wanted? Terrible thoughts I know but my cynicism and black humour was becoming increasingly difficult to tame.

I was surprised to find a marvellous buffet laid on. All the guests - except me - had donated whatever they could to celebrate the occasion. Some had even slaughtered their own chickens, depriving themselves of valuable daily eggs. Others donated wine and liquor and what looked like slices of beef on bread. Probably someone's pet dog but I cared not. The food was consumed in candlelight in the cellar whilst violinists played accompanied by a pianist. The reverberation of nearby shells occasionally broke the beautiful sound of music - but no one cared. The afternoon was one of much needed merriment, as the couple began their very uncertain future.

Sarajevo was a total mess and everything was in short supply. Many people were driven to eat their pets, grass, leaves and anything remotely edible to keep starvation at bay. The electricity supply was virtually non-existent. The city was often cut off from the outside world for weeks at a time, meaning very little in the way of supplies came in. Due to the lack of clean water, hygiene was a continual problem. I had diarrhoea the whole time I was there and considered it normal, along with substantial weight loss. Once a week, electricity permitting, I would boil about six inches of dirty brown water, with my very small kettle, to bathe in; and then wash my clothes in it. In times of severe hardship, I boiled the same water to make tea; adding water purification tablets - just to be safe - and drank it.

Shellfire constantly ruptured the city's water supply pipes, allowing clean water and untreated sewage to mix, encouraging the spread of hepatitis and other water born diseases. This was now becoming a serious problem. The Global Relief Organisation spent considerable time and money renewing the water sanitation system throughout

Sarajevo, with regular flights (when permitted) bringing in new pipes and equipment. This would be promptly installed, then blown up by shells - the process having to start all over again.

In the late summer of 1995, the airlift into the city by the UN resumed. Known as 'Maybe Airlines'. 'Maybe you fly, maybe you don't, maybe you'll get there, and maybe you won't.' This being the comical buzz phrase in circulation at that time.

Flights had been suspended and all roads closed, due to the increasing number of attacks from both Serbian and Croatian anti-aircraft fire on aid aircraft and vehicles. One Italian twin-engined transport plane had been shot down by a surface to air missile whilst on final approach into Sarajevo Airport, killing the crew. Despite assurances from the Serbs, aircraft were often hit by both small arms, and anti-aircraft fire from Serbian gun positions, near to the airport. This served as a reminder of how dangerous it could be to fly in and out of Sarajevo. A subsequent UN investigation revealed that on this occasion - judging by the trajectory of the missile - Bosnian Muslims launched it from nearby positions. They would of course deny this hoping to discredit the Serbs further. I watched with trepidation as aircraft came into land with a morbid anticipation that I could witness the spectacle of one being shot out of the sky.

The aircraft would appear far too high to make a safe landing when on final approach, but quite suddenly and at the last moment, drop suddenly towards the runway - with their undercarriage and flaps fully down. This was known as the 'Khe Sahn' landing, and was developed by the Americans during their ill-fated involvement in Vietnam. The technique allowed supplies to be flown in to beleaguered marines surrounded by the North Vietnamese Army on a large hill at Khe Sahn in northern Vietnam - not dissimilar to our current circumstances. The idea was to keep aircraft out of range of effective small arms fire (about 1500ft) right until the last moment. Incredibly, large transport aircraft, typically Lockheed C130 Hercules, could land, unload, and take off within fifteen minutes, thus minimising exposure to hostile fire whilst on the ground. Sometimes the aircraft barely stopped, as the cargo was unloaded. They always left their engines running.

The threshold of the runway was actually in Serb' held territory with aircraft flying some two hundred feet over them, making a very easy target. On the 11th March '95 one of our aircraft, a twin engined Jet Stream, used for transporting personnel and mail, having just passed the threshold was hit by a burst of anti-aircraft fire. One round narrowly missing the pilot's feet by ten inches, passing through the nose of the aircraft. Fortunately, the damage caused was only minor. The two pilots, both ex South African Air Force, seemed quite proud at having some damage to show for their flights to Sarajevo - no doubt something to talk about in the bars of Zagreb in Croatia where they were based, and tell their grandchildren in the future.

When flying into or out of Sarajevo I always felt relieved once the aircraft had touched down, safe from the threat of being shot out of the sky.

We usually had two incoming flights per day, one by the Jet Stream and the other by a huge Illushin Il-17 transport aircraft, hired by the Global Relief Organisation from a recently formed private Russian company. The crew of the IL-17 largely maintained the aircraft themselves. I admired their ability to keep this old, ex military beast flying. They were often seen stripping parts (risking being shot) off a similar crashed example at the end of the runway - keeping their own in a reasonably air worthy condition. They operated in stark contrast to the safety standards of any western airline.

I regularly drove to the airport to pick up personnel, aid, or general supplies that kept us operational. This could be anything from paper, pens, and computers, to water purification tablets or pipes to repair the damaged sewage system. Whilst on my way to the airport, I was often contacted by radio to tell me the Serbs had just 'temporarily' closed it. Somewhat of an oddity as the airport was supposedly under the control of the UN, being staffed, managed, and operated entirely by UN personnel. However, the Serbs surrounded the airport on three sides with considerable firepower; including multi barrelled anti-aircraft guns and surface to air missiles. I expect the UN could do nothing but comply with the Serbian authorities 'request' to cease operations. The Serbs would quite simply 'fail to guarantee the safety of any incoming flights,' loosely translated, what they really meant was 'We're in charge here and dare you to defy us; we will shoot your aircraft down'. They literally called the shots controlling the flight schedule into and out of Sarajevo Airport. This was to the embarrassment of the airport officialdom. The largely impotent United Nations had to obey, and then negotiate a safe passage, in an ongoing game of brinkmanship. The same was true for the main supply roads in and out of Sarajevo. They were all overlooked by artillery and, to a degree, controlled by the Serbian Army - usually in contest with local Bosnian Army forces.

In early April, the closure of the roads in and out of Sarajevo and airport lasted for about ten weeks.

This made a particularly difficult time for both the population of Sarajevo and aid organisations working within the enclave. Fortunately, the policy of the Global Relief Organisation was to engage with the warring parties, in order to try to maintain a consistent supply chain. It didn't always work, but was far more efficient than the United Nations, who, in my opinion, operated in a more confrontational manner. They seemed to hold a misguided self-assured belief, that they could re-supply themselves without the cooperation of the warring local military commanders: how wrong they were. The United Nations left themselves wide open to literally being starved out of the city in their completely erroneous conviction, that the warring factions had respect for them and allow them to fulfil their UN mandate. The apparent incompetence of the western military and political leadership convinced me that they were in fact, wrestling with the concept of peacekeeping, and what it actually entailed. In fairness to the UN, they were an army trained and equipped to fight a largely defensive war against the former Soviet Union and not equipped for this new role. The UN did not build up stocks of food, water, or diesel when they had the chance earlier on in their deployment. The Global Relief Organisation, and other non-government organisations, were far more competent and skilful in stockpiling essential provisions - leaving nothing to chance.

The Global Relief Organisation, drawing on its vast expertise, knew how fragile a logistical chain could be, and during safer periods, accumulated a vast store of diesel and other essentials, thus allowing operations to continue throughout 'lean' periods. These were stored in several locations all over the city so that a direct hit from a shell on one of the storage areas would not render the Global Relief Organisation ineffective - commonsense really. The United Nations on the other hand, virtually ran out of diesel and had to ask the Global Relief Organisation to help. They wouldn't - not wanting to be seen as anything but impartial.

I felt that the decision not to help the UN might have had repercussions, should the situation have worsened, and us needing their assistance to evacuate. Would they have been so enthusiastic about helping us? I think not. Although I respected the judgement of the Global Relief Organisation, I was uncomfortable with their decision. The UN, under its mandate also acted impartially, although many would argue that this was not always the case.

Back in Sarajevo, our warehouse soon had virtually nothing left to distribute, except a few emergency provisions. The demands of keeping the vulnerable fed throughout the city would quickly exhaust our stocks for distribution, if we did not receive our daily replenishment flights. Nonetheless, we did have a significant amount of cheese that would soon fall beyond the use by date. It was a considerable task to distribute these small ten-ounce blocks to the needy. A ten-ounce block was insufficient for a family, but after having none for three and a half years, it was gratefully received. Some was delivered to the various institutions, particularly hospitals and orphanages.

I felt a moral obligation to continue to do something for the people of Sarajevo as the siege continued to tighten its grip. At that time, a front line hospital in the suburb of Dobrinja was desperate for water. Dobrinja, located on the north side of Sarajevo Airport and had once been the press village during the Winter Olympics of 1984. It had previously been 'cleansed of Muslims' by the Serbs, but had been retaken by the Bosnian BiH and subsequently subjected to regular heavy bombardment by the Serbs. In actual fact, the village was only accessible via a single road, which was constantly under Serbian artillery, mortar and sniper fire. A very dangerous place indeed, and an extremely nerve racking road to drive down. It was foolish to venture on foot into the line of fire - except in an absolute emergency and then for only a few seconds. Anything more than a brief exposure, would almost certainly attract a sniper's bullet. In places, the opposing Serbs were separated by a mere ten yards of territory from the Bosnian Muslim Army. No one in the city would take the risk of keeping the hospital supplied with water but, as I had an armoured truck, which was not an absolute guarantee of safety, I volunteered to undertake this venture. One of our Headquarters administration assistants, who said she would like to come with me to act as my translator volunteered to come with me. I refused her valiant offer as by now I had become sufficiently competant in Serbo-Croat to get by. I did not know her well enough to rely on her if we came under fire. I hadn't forgotten the incident back in Mostar, when the translator completely lost control of herself the year before. Perhaps unfairly, not forgetting the brave female doctors and nurses working on the front line in Sarajevo, I did not want any young women around me if we found ourselves under attack, or if anything untoward was to happen. Perhaps I was sexist but part of me preferred to go alone being only responsible for myself. I was also quite attracted to her and knew that she was to me. We had spent time alone together, and if she was killed, I do not think that I would have gotten over it so easily.

Equipping myself with an eleven hundred gallon water bladder and a pump kindly borrowed from a French aid organisation, I made the journey on a daily basis for about three months.

Normally, I would arrive at the water collection point in the middle of the city at around 8.00 am, queuing with many other vehicles, local authority trucks, all delivering to other parts of the city and their own military units: all legitimate targets as far as the Serbian gunners were concerned. I often wondered what wasn't a legitimate target. We were all 'bunched up' in a queue: it seemed ridiculous to give the Serbian artillery such an easy target but, like the rest of the drivers, if I wanted water I had no choice but to queue. At least there were many 'targets' for the gunners to select from. I hoped that I wouldn't be one of them.

The collection point was an under ground spring, located in an old brewery, previously used to make the local beer, 'Sarajevska' which could be drunk by the dozen and have virtually no effect as it was very weak. The Serbs would often target the brewery with airburst shells. Having a proximity fuse, they would detonate at a predetermined height above the brewery, despatching sharp pieces of red hot metal splinters towards the ground. Incoming shells could be heard and on many occasions, if I had time, I scrambled for cover underneath my truck. In the event of there not being enough time, I simply lay flat on the back of the truck tight against the headboard, hoping not to get hit.

It was prudent to fill the water bladder quickly and leave for the front line. Miraculously the water bladder, exposed on the back of the truck was never punctured.

Shortly after I undertook the water supply duty, I came under unrealistic and ill thought out expectations (both from my management and medical department at headquarters in Sarajevo) to make regular deliveries to predetermined sites throughout the city, thus allowing people to fill up buckets or water containers. I was reluctant to do this, realising that I would make myself a prime target for the overlooking Serb' guns and snipers, lying in wait and within easy range. I also realised how desperate people were, so against my better judgement I cautiously decided to undertake the venture. After all, what was I there for if I was not prepared to take some risks? Sometimes I actually enjoyed risk taking, seeing it as a challenge, much like running the gauntlet to headquarters from the Holiday Inn, when first arriving in Sarajevo - or walking back along Sniper Alley. Maybe the Serb' gunners would not seek to destroy me for something that, it was plain to see was nothing more than a humanitarian exercise? However, I knew this had not stopped them before.

Vojo - the new warehouse supervisor replacing Zorren, with whom I had now become great friends, advised me repeatedly not to go. I never really did comprehend the dangers of what I was doing, until I came home and had time to think about it, but that could be said for the whole venture.

The warehousemen would have my truck prepared and loaded up with the water pump and bladder every morning, ready for me to go to the water collection point. Vojo was the only one who spoke out, continuing to warn me with genuine concern of the dangers and not to go. The other warehousemen looked at me, like the Holiday Inn staff some months before, as though I was already dead. Perhaps I soon would be.

When having parked up in a courtyard, adjacent to a block of flats, having made every effort to shield my truck from Serb' spotters in the surrounding hills, I would uncoil the hose connected to the water bladder. I always ensured that the end where the water exited, was as far away from the truck as possible, thus protecting myself and vehicle from flying shrapnel - should I and the recipients of my cargo be shelled. Shortly after, people emerged from their hiding places; scurrying across open spaces, hoping to take as much of the life sustaining liquid as possible. Squabbles broke out as buckets, watering cans and bottles were filled with the precious fluid. To my relief, the water replenishment on this occasion passed off peacefully. The children used the water bladder as a 'trampoline', helping force the water down the long hose, after I found it would not flow easily. It was very risky to stay stationary in any one location for long. I was glad when the exercise had been completed.

Before leaving, I explained to the people that I had to visit other areas and would come back the next day. I never did make a second trip as at the next location, three mortars fell nearby, scattering all those hoping to obtain water. No one, to my knowledge, was injured or killed, but I left hastily, yet again in a state of adrenaline induced fear. Despite the medical department's protest, I refused to take this unnecessary risk, explaining that I was lucky to be alive and that the inhabitants had previously survived by alternative means. They would have to continue to gather water through the labyrinth of tunnels and culverts that connected collection points, preferably at night, as they had done for the last three years. My decision against continuing to deliver water to individual apartment blocks was made in the broader context of what I felt was my humanitarian objective. Decisions like this might not appear obvious to impoverished, desperate people, or were indeed easy for me to make - but I was there to help en-masse and clearly not the individual. I continued to supply the hospital on a daily basis - this being more sustainable for my nerves!

Numerous people had been killed whilst looking for, or gathering water; often the unfortunate experience of being in the wrong place at the wrong time. If I had inadvertently turned them into 'sitting ducks', dictating the time and place for them to collect their water supplies, I would have had more than a hand in their fate and felt some responsibility for the inevitable deaths that *would* have occurred. I did not want to contribute to their demise, or have a hand in their destiny any more than I already did.

I usually arrived at the hospital mid morning, quickly uncoiling the hose from the truck into the hospital kitchen, pumping some five hundred gallons into the water tank. I then proceeded to fill up the outdoor tank, having to scale ladders running up the side. This tank was often shot at, allowing the water to escape through the holes, which had to be welded by brave local civil workers. Fortunately, the Serbs did not attempt to shoot me whilst climbing the ladders - nevertheless I knew my life was in their hands and felt uneasy when making a connection: half expecting a bullet to hit me in the head or penetrate my body armour and on into my back - a fact I simply could not ignore. I was always very apprehensive perfecting a very swift connection and disconnection of the hose.

On one occasion, the water pump was running at full speed when three mortars landed about twenty yards down the road, demolishing a car and setting the remains of it alight; shattering nearby windows and killing a middle-aged man; whom I can only assume was on his way to beg for water. His left hand still gripped a plastic container. An open brown paper parcel lay near by, exposing a large piece of bread soaked in blood, belonging to another man lying wounded and exposed on the street - hit by the same mortar; whilst no doubt on his way to collect water too - just to survive, I mused.

The wounded man's groans slowly petered out as his lifeblood drained from his body - the sooner the better I thought. There was no way I could go out into the middle of the road to help him without risking being shot. I was there to help en-masse and not the individual - I once again told myself.

Chunks of road and earth landed close by. At the time, I was casually leaning up against the side of my truck daydreaming - transfixed by the sound of the water pump motor. Brought back to reality and needing no further encouragement I jumped onto the back of my truck - now in a fully alert state of mind. Forgetting about the dead people in the road, I fumbled with panicky hands for the off switch on the water pump motor. It was quite difficult to access, as I had strapped the pump to the back of my truck and the switch was, unfortunately, virtually underneath one of the straps. Bad planning on my part - I later thought to myself. In desperation and fear, I again made a conscious effort to remain in control and not just run as my instincts were telling me. Three more mortars landed even closer; my shaking hands fumbled to find the switch - the pump was very hot, and believing the next salvo would land right on top of me, I searched even more frantically for that dammed switch. On finding it, I burnt my hand quite badly on the hot metal casing, but finally managed to shut down the motor. This allowed me to unscrew the high-pressure hose and then jump off the exposed back of the truck and run into my armoured cab. I drove off as fast as I could, leaving the hose spilling valuable unpumped water onto the road.

My hand soon began to blister quite badly and became very painful. I returned to the hospital the next day where the nurses, who noticed my attempt to bandage the burn, took me to a casualty clearance room full of injured soldiers and civilians, needing more prompt attention than myself. They were by now experts at dealing with burns and redressed my hand in clean sterile bandages doused with an opaque, treacle like substance primarily consisting of tea tree oil; a naturally occurring healing substance. This magically provided me with relief from the pain within minutes of being applied. The nurses changed my dressing daily over the following week and seemed only too pleased to pamper me to show their gratitude for the daily water supplies. After my ill fated attempt at getting Eve into bed I quite enjoyed the female attention, prolonging my visits for as long as possible, forgetting the previous days happenings.

Following this latest incident, I sought further ways of enhancing my safety and decided to refill the water bladder in the afternoon, rather than early in the morning. I arranged for armed guard watch over the vehicle over night (clean water being extremely valuable and fetching a high Black Market price), ready for a very early morning delivery.

I would now arrive at the hospital at around 6.00 am, before the mist which settled in the valley, where the hospital was, had had time to clear. Consequently, Serbian artillery spotters would be denied a clear view of the hospital thus allowing my delivery as the 'enemy' slept off the effects of their previous evenings drinking binge. Once the sun rose, it would very quickly burn the mist away, making me once again very vulnerable to sniper or mortar fire. Usually, by then, I should just about be finished and ready to depart the location.

My only remaining concern was that at that time of the morning, the noise of the water pump would easily carry across the sleeping valley and may arouse both Serbian mortar teams and artillery gunners. They would already have the co-ordinates dialled into their weapons from previous attacks on the hospital; they might just decide to shell me anyway. Fortunately, this didn't happen and I was able to replenish the hospital fully without further hindrance. Another valuable lesson learned in my personal 'war of survival'.

People often gathered around my truck, hoping I would fill their water containers. This, I sometimes did but, more often than not, I had to discourage such practice based on my previous experience of Serb' mortar teams; who had already revealed their willingness to target any such congregation of people, or anyone stupid enough to expose themselves unnecessarily. However, there was one exception when a man, about sixty years old, came with two empty Cola bottles asking me to fill them up. As there was no one else around, I thought it would do no harm and quickly filled the bottles up. Such was his gratitude he thrust a small, matchbox-sized hall marked solid gold horseshoe into the palm of my hand. I immediately tried to give it back; he could use this for trading for food, but he was insistent I kept it. He said I must keep it with me to bring me luck and keep me safe. I keep it in my wallet and believe that it has indeed kept me safe.

On June 15th 1995, I was thirty years old and now making my regular early morning trip to the hospital. The hospital staff, whom I had previously made aware of my forthcoming birthday, had very kindly (and expectedly) made me a cake, as a token of their gratitude for my help in keeping the hospital functioning. I was touched.

Returning to the task in hand, I connected the hose to one of the two water tanks, jumped off my truck and was about to walk back into the kitchen area to share the cake. A salvo of three mortar shells landed some fifteen to twenty yards away. The explosion was deafening - really deafening. Amidst the sound of screaming men and women I automatically placing my hands over my ears and threw myself to the ground, just outside the entrance to the kitchen.

'Jesus fuckin' Christ!' I shouted, pleading with him in blasphemy to save me!

I gathered my senses whilst rolling over and glancing over my body to confirm that I hadn't been hit: I hadn't. If there is a God, he was watching over me, I deliberated. Expecting further incoming rounds, I lay motionless on the ground for a few brief moments before picking myself up. There were no further impacts, so I stood up, dusted myself off, and regained my well-practised 'immortal' composure. Upon entering the kitchen, I found my cake sitting, isolated, on a table. Dust filled the room, hanging in the air like a fog of cigar smoke in an exclusive gentlemen's smoke room after an evening of poker. Kitchen staff, a few nurses, and several doctors huddled together for comfort in an adjoining dust filled room, all looking very afraid, waiting for further impacts. That must have been the screaming I had previously heard. We all began to laugh nervously. Then the nurse who had previously tended to my burnt hand came over to me. In faltering English, she wished me happy birthday and kissed my wilting white, dust covered face. I was still in shock from the three mortars: my comfort came not from the companionship shown to me, although the sight of equally frightened doctors and nurses was somehow reassuring, but from the bullet-proof vest and helmet I was wearing. They were my best friends. I took my knife from its sheath, wiped it on my trouser leg, and shared my birthday cake with the remaining staff, who were now once again starting to relax a little and be themselves.

Later, I thought how ironic it would have been to be killed on my birthday. Thirty years to the day!

Eventually, after some weeks, I became terribly anxious about my early morning ventures to Dobrinja Hospital and its potentially life-threatening hazards. The whole experience was grinding me down, making it increasingly difficult to take stock of my once well-managed fears and remain focused. To allay my newfound anxiety, I chose not to associate with anyone the evening prior to, or during the morning before I left for the front line. This helped me to focus my thoughts in letting fate take its course: much as I had done before when lying in the hospital accident unit, after my road accident in 1984.

After the ritual dawn chorus of shelling had subsided, I would make myself a cup of tea, and alone, sneak into one of the eastern facing rooms of the Holiday Inn. On a clear day, I would watch the sun in all its splendour, rise and spread its rays amongst the early morning haze and wounded buildings of Sarajevo. I found peace and solace that only sunrise brings and reflected upon the previous days events - sometimes contemplating the ones ahead. Often rehearsing how I hoped I would react to any given dangerous situation and putting to the back of my mind that, in a few hours, I could quite conceivably be dead: it may have been unlikely - but I certainly felt this way. I was unable to stay drinking tea for long, because of the necessity to be on the road before the protective cloak of mist evaporated.

I quickly learned that surviving in Sarajevo meant that, as the Global Relief Organisation didn't seem to be totally aware of the dangers I faced on the front line, whilst delivering water, that I had to take complete responsibility for my own safety. I remained adamant that if I deemed a particular venture too dangerous, that no 'meant' no. Accordingly, I resisted the continuous pressure to once again deliver water to individual apartment blocks.

My cautious decision-making was later proven to be justified. I was asked to join a convoy over Mount Igman, taking a member of the Global Relief Organisation out of the city and bring another member in. (Mount Igman was a mountain that overlooked Sarajevo and presently held by both Muslim and Croatian forces). The road over the mountain was watched closely by nearby Serbian artillery spotters. At one particular point, known quite simply as 'the danger mile', aid convoys and other vehicles, - some carrying refugees - were shelled and mortared at will by the Serbs. Although this was becoming a fairly common occurrence, the route still proved to be the safest road in and out of the city. Most importantly, written permission wasn't needed from the Serbian authorities to use the road, as it wasn't territory they had direct control of. Personally, I think they resented this and used it as justification for the increasing casualties occurring on the pass.

In war, men can often rely on the support of others facing the same difficulties as themselves, drawing strength from this. In Sarajevo, often working alone, I did not have any such salvation. Three days prior to the proposed trip, I could not sleep. I didn't feel at all comfortable with the idea of making the crossing. Too many vehicles had been hit in the 'danger mile'. I was within my rights to refuse the trip and, on this occasion, after much deliberation, I did. Two colleagues who volunteered to undertake the journey were consequently lucky to escape with their lives. With Global Relief Organisation flags flying from their well-marked Land Rover, they were shelled, as so called, 'legitimate' targets. Shrapnel from mortars hit the BBC Land Rover travelling in front of them, taking the front wing off, and causing considerable bodywork damage. Luckily, no one was injured. The Global Relief Organisation Land Rover wasn't hit, but my colleagues, somewhat distressed by viewing the narrow escape of the BBC Land Rover, right in front of them, blatantly refused to drive back over the mountain. Both of the Global Relief Organisation personal, who originally volunteered to go out, and the new member being brought in, had to wait two weeks until the airlift was resumed - before returning to Sarajevo. Initially, I questioned my well-founded logic about not accepting the trip, though I needn't have. Maybe this was yet another incident of a misplaced sense of ego? However, as a direct consequence of using this crossing, we temporarily lost two important members of staff and an essential vehicle - the losses could have so easily been permanent: I was wholly justified with my concern about making the crossing.

It was important, and indeed Global Relief Organisation policy, to ensure food and medical supplies were distributed according to need, without political or military interference.

From the main warehouse in Sarajevo, once a week, a truckload of mainly medical equipment would be delivered to Pale, seven miles south east of Sarajevo. Pale was where the Bosnian Serb' Army, commanded by Radavan Karadzić, had its Headquarters. Karadzić, formerly a sports psychologist for the former Sarajevo football team, was now the ruthless, self-proclaimed Bosnian Serb' leader. Karadzić was suspected of, and has since been indicted for war crimes; he is believed to be at large somewhere in the region.

The Global Relief Organisation presence in Pale consisted of only two overseas aid workers, both nurses, and two locally employed Serbs, one being a communications specialist and the other an administration assistant. They enjoyed a fairly enviable and peaceful existence and had clean water, food and a reliable electricity supply.

The single truck trips out of Sarajevo to Pale were very much sought after. Hans and I would take it in turns, travelling alone, usually carrying medical supplies. Initially, I was rather unsure of undertaking the trip alone. As usual, and for no apparent reason, I made a mental note of positions of anti-aircraft gun emplacements, locations, and types, as I crossed the lines. Even the apparent quality of troops was something that I began to take an interest in. I also remained aware at all times that local militia operated in the area - and just how dangerous it could be. Occasionally, we would make a two-truck journey but this was certainly not the norm, which was unfortunate, as I remained fearful of the realistic and ever present danger of ambush and felt better if there were two targets, or at least two of us to work through any 'situation'. The lure of leaving the cramped, depressing surroundings of the battered city proved too much and a risk well worth taking - alone or otherwise. It was indeed a refreshing experience travelling through the 'empty' green, fresh smelling countryside, surrounding the claustrophobic dismal city. Having passed through Bosnian Muslim checkpoints and across a very dangerous section of No-Mans-Land, into the 'Republic of Srbska', the stark contrast between bombed out Sarajevo, and the beautiful countryside surrounding the capital, impacted upon me greatly. The route to Pale took me into the hills surrounding Sarajevo, which were lined with beautiful evergreen fir trees; providing a false sense of protection and security. In fact, they provided ideal cover for the militia or anyone with a grudge against the Global Relief Organisation to mount an ambush, or hijacking. This was forgotten as I filled my lungs with the fresh clean fragrance of pine, which wafted in full glory through the air vents of my truck.

On one of the rare occasions that both Hans and I both went to Pale, and whilst crossing No-Mans-Land, Hans, driving in front abruptly stopped his truck. I too slammed on my brakes. I thought he had spotted a mine or something and tried to call him on the radio. It wasn't safe to stop between front lines. He didn't respond. A few seconds later and to my amazement, he ran between the trucks, dropped his trousers, leant up against the back of his lorry and defecated. I thought what an idiot he was doing that here in full view of the opposing military forces. I soon began to laugh at him as he looked up at me rather sheepishly with his trousers around is ankles. He had obviously succumbed to yet another bout of diarrhoea. I expect the soldiers hidden in their trenches were also laughing. He really was caught with his trousers down!

Serbian soldiers, typically served two weeks on the front line and two weeks off, living in very primitive conditions, manning the guns and dug in tanks overlooking Sarajevo. Cooking by these soldiers was forbidden, as tell tale columns of smoke would reveal their camouflaged positions. Winter in the hills was particularly harsh and cold - they were not even allowed to make a hot drink. Frostbite caused more casualties amongst these freezing soldiers than the regular suicidal incursions by Bosnian Special Forces.

Contrary to popular belief conjured up by the press, on the whole, Serbian artillery gunners surrounding Sarajevo weren't a 'blood thirsty bunch of savages', but more often middle-aged men who privately wanted this hell to end as much as the people they were ordered to shell. It didn't need highly trained or indeed highly motivated artillerymen to fire their guns into Sarajevo on a daily basis: it was impossible to miss; being right at the end of the gun barrels. Most of the artillerymen, operating these heavy guns, quite simply wanted to go home. They didn't hate the people of Sarajevo; most of them, in fact, had many friends trapped in the city and would constantly ask me about people whom I didn't know, or whose name I had little chance of remembering - should I have ever met them.

The gunners and tank crews were usually friendly towards me. They knew I was bringing in medical supplies and equipment to assist *their* people. I purposely made friends with them and often stopped for a break to socialise with them, knowing that in a few hours' time, I would be cursing them as they laid down a carpet of shells on the city. Any one of which could snatch my life away in an instant; once having returned to Sarajevo: nothing personal I would remind myself.

Once in the safety of Pale, a small town set in a low valley, and out of the sound of reverberating gunfire, it was simply wonderful to take off my flak-jacket and helmet, and work outside without the fear of being shot or hit by shrapnel. A massive sense of relief and freedom would temporarily engulf me. I enjoyed listening to the birds sing; children shouting in excitement, whilst playing (a sound I would normally do everything possible to avoid - preferring a quiet existence) and breathing the beautiful smokeless, clean air. I would sit on a balcony of the Global Relief Organisations' house, overlooking a stunning green, un-shelled field and unspoilt wooded area. I never thought something as simple as a green field could bring so much pleasure. A great burden lifted from my shoulders. I enjoyed the temporary privilege of escaping Sarajevo and made the best of it. Trees, not only stood proud and upright, but still had their branches and foliage intact. It made me feel quite human as I felt the internalised stress of Sarajevo easing from my body…

Staff at the small assignment were only too aware of the pressure on those working in the city, and went out of their way to make us visiting 'escapees' welcome. They would cook a nourishing pasta and meat meal and pander to our every whim. A hot meal with flavour, served on a real plate, and eaten with a knife and fork! I had almost forgotten… They were able to acquire virtually any foodstuff via Greater Serbia, and lived very well in their unbelievably contrasting world.

The medical supplies were unloaded into a nearby warehouse, which was within sight of the luxurious home of Karadzić - and his entourage of armed guards: just a few miles away, the people of Sarajevo were forlorn, sick, and starving.

The Serbs thought that these supplies were for them, but they were in fact intended for nearby Muslim enclaves such as Srebrnica, whose population had now swollen from nine thousand to some fifty thousand inhabitants. Refugees continued to flee from other, already fallen towns. Srebrnica was bearing up to the continuing siege conditions at the hands of the Serbs having received no supplies of any kind for many weeks, causing unimaginable depravation. Surgical operations were performed without anaesthetic; on both adults and children alike. In Pale and nearby hospitals there was no shortage of medicines.

However, the Serbs soon learned that the supplies were not for them and consequently would not allow us to make deliveries to any of the enclaves. They said that it was too unsafe and they couldn't 'guarantee our safety'. (They would, at best, turn our convoys away or, at worst threaten our destruction). The reality is that they were still destroying Srebrnica, and a further eight thousand of its male adult population, in a programme of 'ethnic cleansing'. They were marched to a nearby woods and cold bloodily murdered by lining them up alongside pre dug pits and shot, one at a time, in the back of the neck. Some of the men escaped, but were hunted down and shot like wild boar, or re-captured and their throats cut: to the sound of jeering Serbian troops. In the knowledge that their men folk were dead, I heard of mothers smothering their young children, as they slept, so as not to become bayonet practice for the invading troops. Stories leaked from Srebrnica, via local radio transmissions, pleading for help. They spoke of women who had hanged themselves, to avoid the trauma of being raped or killed, or both. Apparently, no one in Srebrnica had any faith in the once again ineffective UN force who were there to protect them. Due to restraints placed upon them, the UN had no option but to negotiate with the Serbs in a seemingly face saving exercise. This turned out to be an embarrassing climb down for what many now considered an impotent and directionless United Nations.

In July 1995, as anticipated, the Serbs overran the 'safe area' of Srebrnica. They were keen to assuage western condemnation and laid on coaches to evacuate women and children who wanted to leave. The few remaining men who had escaped execution were not allowed onto the coaches. Between seven and nine thousand men and teenage boys remain, to this day, unaccounted for. Investigators are currently exhuming many mass graves, spotted by American satellites, in the woods surrounding Srebrnica. Was this a mini-holocaust all over again? The rest of the world looked on as this butchery took place - but shamefully did little else.

The Serbs quite simply kept the Global Relief Organisation - and other organisations out. They did not want anyone to witness the slaughter, atrocities, and starvation that was taking place. Consequently, a vast amount of much needed medicines and equipment, as well as flour, rice and beans, stood idly rotting in a warehouse as the enclaves bled and starved to death.

Another occasional trip out of Sarajevo was to the Serbian-held water pumping station - some five miles away. This was manned, and commanded, largely by Serbian soldiers. It supplied water to the whole of the city, including the Muslim sectors and United Nations bases. It was impossible for the Serbs to supply water to the Serb' sectors of the city alone, without supplying the Muslim sectors at the same time. The Global Relief Organisation provided chemicals that would help make the water safe; along with the technical expertise and water pipes - to replace pipes constantly damaged by shelling.

The Serbs used the fact that they supplied the Bosnian Muslim sectors to gain maximum propaganda value, in an effort to demonstrate a humane side to 'their' war. This was despite regularly turning the water off, which in fact meant Serbian people would also be without. They, nevertheless, felt it necessary to demonstrate who was in charge.

One of the senior military men at the pumping station spoke English and enjoyed practicing it with me. He would take his cherished Magnum out of its holster and place it on the table (a Serbian sign of good intention), whilst we both drank Slivovitz.

He spoke in graphic detail of how, earlier on in his 'war career', he had killed many Bosnian Muslims, including women and children, describing how, on one occasion, he removed a baby from the womb of a live pregnant woman whilst she screamed. Other like-minded soldiers held her down. With nothing more than a knife and bare hands, which he used to gesticulate his actions, he described how the baby was removed. The woman's screams and resistance subsiding as she died: the dead baby held high - like a trophy from a sporting event. He laughed as he drew his hands down the front of his uniform indicating how he was covered in the dead baby's blood; proud of his sadistic achievement, in the strange misconception that I should also be impressed. I formed the impression that being based at the water pumping station made him feel undervalued, as he was not able to continue his reign of terror. I made no response and showed no emotion. His eyes portrayed a chilling evilness I had never seen before - and never want to see again. To him, killing was an enjoyable experience and one to relish - if only to prove your manhood. I continued to listen impassively, making no comment throughout; thinking how I would quite happily kill this man for what he had done.

As he became more and more drunk, I anxiously began to eye the loaded pistol on the table. Alcohol and guns don't mix. He had no reason to kill me, did he? I shouldn't be nervous, and if I am, I mustn't show it - I thought to myself. I quietly hoped that, after the war, he would be indicted for war crimes, but for now, for the sake of others, I had to appease and work with this most evil of men.

More than a decade on, I still feel as though I would like to kill him.

Chapter Nine

Sarajevo was becoming desperate. The civilian population of all factions were becoming increasingly agitated, with both the United Nations and its own army for their lack of success in lifting the siege of Sarajevo. Over recent months, the BiH had built up its strength. There were many soldiers in the city, particularly near the BiH Headquarters. Morale was high; all now very well equipped and motivated to finally free the city. An atmosphere of optimism prevailed over the troops.

The Bosnian Black Swan soldiers who had recently arrived from Tuzla, after having being stationed there to train and build up strength, were a highly trained, apparently elite force, numbering several thousand. They had entered Sarajevo via Mount Igman: still the only route allowing passage into the city without encroaching Serbian controlled territory. The road over the mountain and surrounding area remained largely in Bosnian Muslim control, in conjunction with aligned Croatian forces. The Serbs could still shell the majority of it at will, but it nevertheless proved to be an essential lifeline for Sarajevo and a thorn in the side of Serbian forces. Each member of the Black Swan would have crawled through the three feet square tunnel under the main Sarajevo Airport runway, dragging his allegedly, American supplied equipment into the Muslim sector of Sarajevo.

It was generally accepted that the Americans had been supplying them with equipment, including new Russian-made mortars and large calibre machine guns - bought on the open market. I heard many accounts of United States Air Force Hercules C130 transport planes, flying 'black ops' (illegal arms deliveries), landing at Tuzla Airport to the north of Sarajevo, in the dead of night, quickly unloading their cargo, then disappearing swiftly into the darkness.

The sole mission of the Black Swan was to break the siege of Sarajevo. Part of their objective being to capture and hold the Main Supply Route (MSR), running along the ridge of Mount Bjelasnica, which was defended by well-equipped and entrenched Serbs. Should they be successful, the Bosnian Muslim forces would be able to use the road to supply both themselves and the city's inhabitants with food and ammunition, and at the same time disrupt Serbian logistics. The Serbs anticipated an attack - having strengthened their already strong positions. Sniping, and in particular shelling was on the increase. Looking from my office between the thick steel plates, draped over spaces where windows had once been, offering protection from lurking snipers (a mere hundred and fifty yards away) I had full view of the impending battle.

Overnight, towards the end of June, a large force of Black Swan moved forward in silence to the base of Mount Bjelasnica. Radio traffic kept to an absolute minimum, silently they took up positions in and around a wooded area, adjacent to the Serb' front line trenches.

At first light, and quite suddenly, supported by heavy machine gunfire and mortars, the Black Swan troops streamed out of the woods in a ferocious hard-hitting attack: hoping to take the defenders by surprise. Firing, moving, firing, moving, in a well-rehearsed set piece assault; quickly climbing the hillside to infiltrate the Serb' trenches. To their left and right, Rocket Propelled Grenades slammed into Serbian machine gun nests. Anti-aircraft artillery, strategically located, ripped into the Serb' lines - tracking up and down the trenches, obliterating personnel and everything in its path - keeping the heads of the surviving Serbs down as the Black Swan attacked. The mortars from behind the woods also laid waste to many Serbian soldiers. This is it, I thought, the Black Swan either lift the siege of Sarajevo; or are completely broken as a fighting force.

The Black Swan pushed on. The now awakened and fully alert Serbs, recovering from the shock of the initial attack, began to return a steady stream of fire into the attacking troops, causing many casualties. If they hadn't reacted promptly, they would be completely overrun. In the process, cutting down many of the assaulting troops of the Black Swan.

Serb' mortars began to fall on the wooded area, where the attackers were emerging - killing many BiH soldiers, long before they could even exit the woods and make their final assault.

Still they came - into a ferocious volley of Serbian fire. I was just under a mile away from the hillside, watching the battle unfold through my binoculars. The scenes reminded me of a 1980s Vietnam War movie, Hamburger Hill. A true story where numerous US marines lost their lives assaulting Viet-Cong positions on the top of a hill - themselves being cut to pieces. I had watched it just before leaving home. This wasn't cinema - this was reality.

Some of the soldiers that were hit sagged to the ground in slow motion - as though they had just given up. Others threw their arms out, no doubt letting out a death-defying scream as they tumbled into the muddy earth. At times, the BiH took part of the trench system, only to be beaten back, not by infantry, which the Serbs didn't have much of, but by heavy Serbian artillery; which came into play in overwhelming quantities, decimating the attacking troops and any gains they made. Fierce fighting, some of which was hand-to-hand, continued throughout the day.

At the end of the day - after many lives were lost on both sides, the tactical deployment of troops remained the same as at the beginning of the day. Stalemate: all that death and killing for nothing… I viewed No-Mans-Land through my powerful binoculars and saw scores of young soldiers, many dead. The wounded from both sides were united in their suffering; barely moving, clinging onto life with nothing more than thoughts of their mothers, wives, or girlfriends, to comfort them. I felt both sickened and grateful. Sick at the sight of dying men and grateful that it wasn't me. My heart was in my throat and I felt ashamed of my morbid fascination as I watched this scene of carnage unfold, unable to put the binoculars down as I witnessed history being made: not on television, but here and now, as it happened before my eyes.

The second day brought another Black Swan offensive, much the same as the first day. However, this time carrying on throughout the night. After many more casualties as a result of bitter trench fighting, the Serbian front line trenches were taken. The remaining Serbs abandoned what was left of their equipment, and took up position in support trenches, a short distance behind the front line: in a good defensive position.

 Accurate Serbian heavy artillery carpeted the area, swiftly killing the latest occupants of the newly won trenches. The BiH had no counter battery artillery to reply with and, once all the BiH were killed, or had abandoned the trenches, somewhat broken and disillusioned, the Bosnians made their way back to their own lines. The remaining Serbs simply re-occupied their battered, ethnically mixed, corpse-laden positions.

On day three, the exhausted soldiers of the now depleted Black Swan were unable to mount a successful attack - despite trying. They were a decimated, spent force, fit only for static defence. However, in frustration, both sides took to shooting up the United Nations outpost overlooking No-Mans-Land, separating the two sides. The outpost was a very heavily sand bagged, dug in bunker, situated at the top of a hill, with a commanding view of the battlefield. It became the target of small arms fire and Rocket Propelled Grenades. Occasionally, the few UN soldiers occupying the post would fire back in a gesture of defiance. Their tactical situation was hopeless. They were very lightly armed, isolated and completely beyond rescue. The bunker just about survived the three days of assault, but I am unsure as to the fate of its occupants.

Sarajevo was to suffer retribution by the Serbs for this ill-fated attack. Hundreds of shells fell throughout the next few days, while sniping escalated with a determined and renewed vigour. There was nothing else to do but to sit tight and wait for their anger to abate.

The fall of the so-called 'safe havens' of Zepča and Srebrnica and other besieged enclaves, at the hands of the Serbs, instilled confidence in the Serbian High Command that any intense bombardment of Sarajevo, would continue to be met with nothing more than a UN verbal protest, or token air strike. I believe that this confidence alone encouraged more sustained and aggressive attacks on Sarajevo. On more violent days in the city and surrounding suburbs, casualties could quite easily amount to some three hundred people killed and wounded.

The Serbs had introduced a new weapon, more deadly than shells: a 500 lb aircraft bomb, adapted to enable rocket motors to propel it high into the sky before falling earthwards. This very powerful and lethal contraption would quite easily annihilate a large apartment block and all of its inhabitants - with one hit or near miss.

'Where is the United Nations Protection Force?' The Saralije would ask me. My reply would be nothing more than a 'Dunno' accompanied with a customary shrug of the shoulders. Despite the professionalism displayed by some units - I personally had very little faith in the capabilities and motivation of the majority of the UN protection force.

Although this new weapon was a very real threat, I didn't really care and just wanted to survive my contract with my sanity reasonably intact.

During the three-day battle, I managed to maintain an eleven hundred gallons per day water delivery to the front line hospital at Dobrinja. They needed every drop. I witnessed at first hand the butchery that had taken place, as the hospital overflowed with wounded and dying soldiers - dragged off the battlefield broken and torn. My horror at scenes of young mangled human life will remain with me for the rest of my life. I will never forget the hopeless, but nevertheless determined faces of the overwhelmed hospital staff, in their determination to save these precious young lives. It was utterly dreadful.

The tragic and nauseous sight of wounded soldiers disturbed me as they were brought in on bloodied stretchers. Some were unconscious, some murmuring illegible words from bloody vomit filled mouths, as they lapsed in and out of a semi-comatose state - breathing in short shallow gasps. Others, in shock, stared blankly in disbelief at the part of their body that had recently been reduced to pulp, unable to comprehend what had happened to them. Many of the dead were barely recognisable as human beings. Their green combat fatigues soaked with rich red blood that had not yet had time to darken with age. Tatters of uniform hung, along with outstretched arms, from stretchers as they were brought to the hospital. Some burnt black, probably by phosperous grenades; their remaining flesh resembling freshly made road tar. It was difficult to remain strong and not to break down and weep. I rubbed and closed my now widened eyes, dazed by the carnage. The body of a young Bosnian soldier, about seventeen years old, lay on a stretcher at the foot of my ladders that I used to connect the hose to the water tank. I looked over his body, starting with his feet. His laces neatly tied and his boots polished. Probably cleaned them that very morning and killed on his way to the front line for the first time. Soldiers serving on the front line would never have time or the will for such niceties. As my eyes were drawn further up the corpse, I noticed a gaping hole, the size of a man's fist in his chest: the neatly tied laces left more of an impact upon me… I thought of those boots every time I laced my own boots up for some weeks to come. Tragedies like this boy's death were a common everyday occurrence but I still wasn't used to it. In my numbed state of 'physical disassociation' and somewhat slower than normal, I uncoiled the water hose ready for connection and primed the water pump for delivery.

When making a delivery and trying to remain focused on the task in hand, two mortar shells landed nearby, quickly bringing me to my senses, causing further shrapnel damage to the side panels of the truck. I lay flat on the deck of the truck, preparing for eternity; hoping that any flying shrapnel wouldn't hit me.

'Please God, don't let there be any more.' I shouted with my hands firmly pressed over my ears. Luckily, there was no more. Just a brief reminder from the Serbs that they were in charge and that I should respect and acknowledge that very fact - which I did. I presumed that they were telling me not to hang around for too long, or they would make a more determined effort to kill me.

'Yes sir, I will hurry, and I accept your authority,' I grudgingly said out loud.

I knew that they could accurately drop a salvo right on top of me any time that they wanted to, and duly accepted their warning. I hurried with my task and continued to acknowledge my humble status. The day's supply was delivered successfully; but only after another brush with death had just passed by.

Maybe the experience of being largely responsible for my own well-being throughout my childhood and teenage years, served as a rehearsal for a life of self-reliance in a war zone. I had learned as a youngster when to keep my head down and when not to challenge authority. At least not until circumstances were in my favour: whereupon I would relish any opportunity to emerge from non-entity, and assert myself as a *human being*. This, coupled with the desensitising process that I had undergone in recent months and days, helped me to carry on with my duties; despite all that was taking place around me.

In the aftermath of the battle, once the dust had settled and each side exhausted by combat, the Global Relief Organisation resumed normal distribution services to outlying villages.

One such village, Butmir, commonly known as 'Chicken Village' was, despite constant shelling and intensive sniping, (being so near to the front line) alive with a thriving Black Market. Goods were smuggled in over the lines from Croatia, enabling a semblance of normality to prevail.

Although nothing was ever proved, or any action taken, the local Bosnian Administrator responsible for the distribution of supplies was suspected of corruption by other members of staff. Personally, I found him hard working and conscientious and had no reason to suspect him of any wrong doing. Anyway, he lavished Hans and myself with freshly cooked chicken pieces, accompanied with chicken kidney soup, something of a delicacy in Bosnia - or so I'm told and served only to close family and friends. It had a strong bitter taste and I certainly would not have eaten it at home, but acknowledged that it contained many important vitamins that I needed - and at least varied my otherwise boring diet! I even got to like it after a few hearty bowls! I never asked where the ready supply of chickens came from. Most people in Butmir hadn't eaten fresh meat for the last three years!

The local volunteers would unload the lorries of rice, flour, tinned vegetables etc, into a store attached to the administrator's house. This gave the Administrator the privileged role of 'Village Chief'. He had control of the distribution of food and seemingly, like others in authority in this region, looked after those in his favour. Other Global Relief Organisation officials told us they had heard he was selling a significant amount of the food on the Black Market and making a small fortune. If this was the case, I reasoned that I might well have done the same in his position, in return for others providing me with things that would make my life more bearable. It was estimated that 20% of all goods supplied ended up on the Black Market one way or another. I for one did not consider it a major problem. Food was getting into peoples' stomachs, and there was still enough for the most vulnerable and poor citizens of 'Chicken Village'.

The Global Relief Organisation also delivered food, reading, and writing materials to all orphanages around in and around Sarajevo.

A Serbian orphanage located in Hrasnica, to the north of Sarajevo, housed in what was left of a local school, received its own separate supply of food. It was quite some distance away from our normal storage warehouse and facilities. The beneficiaries were mostly teenagers. However, there were a number of much younger children living there as orphans, being looked after by the older ones. They always came out to thank us for our efforts. I felt quite sorry for them admiring their spirit; as they trudged around in ankle deep mud that was once a playing field, now cratered with shell holes, helping unload the trucks and carry provisions into their nearby storage buildings.

As the number of casualties rose, peaking at around sixty-two thousand of the original six hundred and eighty thousand inhabitants of Sarajevo, (half being children), orphanages became home and family for many of the young.

Whilst at one of the city orphanages, I clearly remember a little girl staring at me. She looked around four years old and carried a black adult's handbag. Her dark shoulder length hair fell scruffily onto her red coat, hiding her pale complexion. She had red lipstick smudged around her mouth as she stood at the gated entrance to the orphanage, staring up at this strange man wearing a white helmet and a green flak

- jacket. I felt that her wide dark brown eyes betrayed some hidden pain that she was too young to understand. I wanted to reach out to her to offer some comfort; but this would have jeopardised the months I had spent purposely becoming detached from such emotion: I wasn't going to let go. I asked an adult member of the orphanage staff, in my broken English-Serbo-Croat, why this empty looking child seemed more lost than the others. The staff member told me that both her mother and father, like so many, had been killed during shelling. This little girl's parents had died only days before... I walked over to her, taking off my helmet. Crouching down beside her, I took her tiny little hands and placed them in my own, in an effort to offer some comfort. She looked up at me, accepting my gesture. What could I do? She didn't move away or seem at all frightened of me, which was reassuring. For a few moments, I felt, and was overcome with a natural desire to help these poor children. Unable to afford the luxury of emotion in war, I got up, slipped my helmet back onto my head, and got to grips with reality. The child looked on.

This particular orphanage looked as though it had once been a home to a wealthy family before the war. Located on a hill in the Muslim part of the city and overlooking Serbian controlled suburbs of Sarajevo made it extremely vulnerable to incoming shells.

There were pleasant gardens with worn down grassed play areas, rusty swings and a rickety seesaw. Most of the children looked underfed with clothes hanging off them, but nevertheless surprisingly active - despite apparent malnutrition. They played with toys and chased each other around the gardens, in and out of the buildings, always under the careful watch of the white-coated female staff, seemingly oblivious to their siege-like existence - and the war. The three and four year olds had known nothing for their entire life but the sound of incoming and outgoing shells, guns, anti-aircraft cannons and now surface-to-surface rockets. Surely, they would be affected for life? How could they not be? They were also starved, despite the efforts of the staff, of parental love and care.

I had tears in my eyes as I left this particular orphanage; realising that the emotional flak-jacket I was wearing was not as immune to the consequence of war as I had previously thought. I promised myself that before leaving Bosnia, I would endeavour to do a little something extra for the orphanage - just to make life a little more bearable for the children and staff. I wasn't sure what or how, but *anything* to make life a little more comfortable.

By now, due to the intensity of shelling, most of the Global Relief Organisation staff had been evacuated to the safety of Split in Croatia. Only essential staff remained. Hans and I, much to our disappointment, were considered essential. In the event of the collapse of Bosnian Muslim defences and the city subsequently being overrun, we would be needed to load as much Global Relief Organisation equipment as possible onto the trucks, and make our own way to Croatia (if we had time). Our only protection being our status as aid workers. From my experience of war, I doubt this operation would have been successful, or if we would have even made the outer perimeter of the city, without being ambushed and slaughtered by conquering Bosnian Serbian troops - or irate Bosnian Muslims for deserting them.

In reality, and at that time unknown to us, this was an unrealistic prospect. Despite the overwhelming superiority in armament, the Serbs, quite simply, did not possess the manpower to mount such an operation. They instead chose one of the oldest but one of the most effective weapons of war: starve the city into submission.

With now only six of the original twenty-two overseas aid staff left, Headquarters seemed eerily empty. Was this an indication of things to come? Was the Global Relief Organisation considering leaving altogether? At the time, I believe it was.

Children, shot on the streets of Sarajevo is something I shall never really come to terms with. On one of the 'sniper safe back streets', people were shot on a daily basis; nobody knew from which direction. Two children, about seven years of age, were riding their bicycles on one of the back streets, having fun. A sniper shot one, sending his young body crashing into the wall as his cycle fell to the ground. There was no time to react before the other child, mesmerised by what he had just seen, and frozen with fear, met a similar fate. A privately owned Zastava car raced forward to help - the driver risking his own life. However, there was no point. The bodies lay lifeless on the road - bathed in each other's blood. Other pedestrians shouted and screamed with terror as they fled the area.

The next day, and from then on, a Ukrainian UN armoured personnel carrier escorted people across the road, its armoured chassis sheltering them from the sniper. Terrified pedestrians cowered beside it, as the vehicle traversed back and forth all day at walking pace. The gunman was ultimately located a mile away in a room at the top of a block of flats in the Serb' sector, and the threat subsequently eliminated by French Legionnaire snipers.

All sides regularly targeted youngsters playing in the suburbs of Sarajevo. Muslim snipers also shot Serbian children, although we did not hear much of this, due to spending much of our time *in* Muslim areas. Serbian snipers shot Muslim children virtually every day in Sarajevo. It really wasn't news any more...

The destruction of Sarajevo and its painfully innocent children was simply a further indication of the self-perpetuating cycle of violence that was endemic on all sides throughout the whole of Yugoslavia. The respect the young and innocent attracted in previous wars by combat troops was not at all evident in the Balkans. This fact in particular, set it aside from conflicts that had taken part in this region previously in the twentieth century. All ethnic groups were guilty of murdering the young - justifying these actions with a 'genocidal' desire to eradicate a particular group of people. Whilst in one of the suburbs, and tentatively speaking to a man carrying a sniper's rifle with a large telescopic sight, I asked him why snipers intentionally killed so many children. He explained to me, that it was an insurance policy to safeguard the future of their own children against further conflict, once they had *won* the war. I didn't labour the point further. Although seemingly amiable, he was after all armed, possibly unpredictable, *and* used to killing. This attitude, I felt, coupled with an overriding need for revenge, would consequently outweigh any desire for peace that the warring parties may have had. In fact, I don't believe any group wanted peace in the accepted sense - they wanted victory and *nothing* less.

Chapter Ten

Life in Sarajevo was measured in inches, as shrapnel routinely killed people and scarred buildings and streets. Death continued to lose all sense and meaning to me; becoming a mere inconsequential facet of war. The population inspired me with its ability to maintain life as normal as possible. The resilience of everyday people in the besieged enclave proved quite remarkable. They risked their lives going to cafés, which had little to offer except black coffee and patak. They also ventured out to buy a locally published newspaper, called Oslobodenje (Freedom). This was simply a news sheet, published weekly, and primarily written to boost the morale of the inhabitants of the besieged city.

The only other news available was rumour. This would range from the totally absurd, to the reasonably feasible - all having to be largely ignored. However, rumour seemed to have had a virtual monopoly on public opinion in Sarajevo.

There were no batteries available to power radios, where more reliable, perhaps balanced news from neutral countries could be heard. Rumour, along with food and water shortages dominated daily conversation.

Trees were cut down in winter to keep warm, albeit the remaining few that were left. Individual pages of precious books were moistened and then almost allowed to dry, thus allowing them to burn more slowly, prolonging what little heat it gave.

The Bosnian conflict was as disturbing as it was gruesome: a war fought in the so-called sophisticated 90s with 1940s technology, imbued with a barbaric medieval mentality.

Shelling was ongoing and sniping particularly cruel. Everyone, including aid workers and journalists, were potential targets and prone to battle fatigue as much as soldiers. In fact, more journalists were killed in the four years of the Bosnian conflict than in the whole of the ten-year war in Vietnam. Twenty-two reported as killed and four recorded as missing, presumed dead in the first nine months alone. Around fifty journalists in total were killed, from the initial outbreak of fighting in Slovenia until the end of hostilities in December 1995. Martin Bell was himself injured by shellfire on the streets of Sarajevo. Indeed, it was rumoured, and probably true that there was a three hundred Deutschemark reward, for any journalist shot and killed by a Serbian sniper: such was the hatred demonstrated by the Serbs, for the exposure they had received for their conduct in the war. In reality, all sides were guilty of atrocities and all utilised snipers, valuing their own snipers as much as they feared their enemies.

During the last days of my six months in the city, bullets and shrapnel were to strike my vehicle on no less than four occasions; immobilising two of our valuable trucks. One such incident, when, after arriving back to the comparative safety of the warehouse, after my regular water delivery to the hospital, six shells landed in quick succession in the yard where the trucks were parked. I was in the process of removing the water pump from the back of my truck to take it into the warehouse, for safe keeping, when the first one of the six shells landed a mere twelve or so yards away in the soft earth of the nearby railway embankment - creating a deafening bang. I briefly caught sight of one of the white and orange flashes of an explosion. Fortunately, the embankment absorbed most of the impact. I was very lucky not to have been hit by the thousands of

Sugar Coated War

flying splinters of shrapnel that momentarily filled the air around me cutting into surrounding buildings and trucks.

It was truly a miracle that I was not slain. Yet again, God was watching over me, protecting me from the ills of war. The compression and explosions from the shells shattered windows on nearby buildings, along with the mirrors of all the vehicles in the courtyard. I was left stunned and completely disorientated; struggling like a wounded animal on the deck of the truck, trying to get up and regain composure. It was all so incredibly loud and violently quick.

Once back on my feet, I realised in my confusion that Vojo was shouting to me, gesturing from the entrance of the warehouse to come inside. I looked closely at him but could not hear anything.

'What? What yer sayin?' I shouted back, in my confusion repeating myself over and over.

Another salvo of shells fell in my vicinity, further adding to my confusion. My ears were ringing and by now, the exploding shells registered in my ears as nothing more than distant crumples in the background. Nothing Vojo said made sense; momentarily in my complete bewilderment I wasn't even sure if I was alive - was this a dream that couldn't possibly be happening?

Vojo disappeared out of my thoughts as an irrational, defiant sense of urgency took over me. I continued to drag the heavy water pump off the truck in a senseless gesture of defiance directed towards whoever was shelling us. I noticed water was gushing out of the truck parked next to me. Shrapnel had entered the engine compartment and had punctured the radiator. The front of the cab and engine compartment irreversibly damaged. Initially I stared at it wondering why it was leaking, still failing to realise what had happened. I clearly wasn't thinking properly and was obviously in a state of shock, forgetting that I could be cut to pieces at any moment. My perception of danger clearly distorted. The pump just had to be taken into safety - as the bombardment continued around me. Nothing seemed more important at the time, although this should have been the lowest of my immediate priorities. My irrational behaviour was due to a combination of shock, mild concussion, and confusion due to the noise and blast of impacting shells. Once I had removed the pump off the truck and into safety, I took cover myself, along with Vojo into the thinly corrugated roofed warehouse. This was no cover at all really; but standing with colleagues, as when been shelled at the hospital in Dobrinja previously, offered its own sort of protection, in a comforting kind of way. Only now did I begin to regain my composure.

A man in his early thirties staggered into our warehouse, blood oozing through his hair, down his neck and onto his shirt. His pupils were dilated and he appeared dazed. I thought maybe a piece of shrapnel had sliced the top of his scalp, leaving a jagged and bloody two-inch gash. Shells were now falling more heavily than before but despite this, and in an act of compassion; I ran across the open courtyard to where my armoured Land Rover was parked, grabbing the comprehensive first aid kit that all our vehicles carried. After running back, again lucky to not get hit and somewhat out of breath as adrenaline again surged through my veins, I gave the bag to Hans, who was a fully trained paramedic and had been calmly sitting on a stool nearby. He quickly sat the man down on his stool and applied a field dressing. The man was in shock and bleeding lightly from his head. Hans told to me that the scalp is served by capillaries and will ooze blood rather than bleed heavily. It just looks messy. However, we didn't know if shrapnel had damaged or pierced his skull. Hans knew best. I'd done my bit. The unknown man was in shock and thought he was going to die. He started to speak rapidly in his native tongue. I didn't know if the injury was serious or not but nonetheless told him he was okay, reassuring him he wasn't going to die. We decided to take him to the local hospital in the back of the Land Rover. We informed Headquarters by radio of our intentions and, in turn, they advised us to use the back streets, as the roads nearest the front line were being shelled; this wasn't actually the case and we drove straight into a 'gridlock' situation. There weren't many cars in Sarajevo but every single one of them seemed to be on the same road as us. These streets were being shelled hard. People fled in confusion, causing complete mayhem and panic. All vehicular movement on the narrow roads simply ground to a halt. We could not go forwards or backwards, as vehicles behind us refused to budge. No one knew what to do or where to go. Drivers seemed to be in a panic-induced freeze.

White phosphorous shells passed overhead falling on the hillside on the outer edge of the city, creating large white and deceivingly pretty mushroom clouds. Fortunately, this area wasn't heavily populated, but anyone caught in the streaks of phosphorous that spewed out from each explosion, would have been horribly burnt. The chemical burrows feverishly and deeply into the skin. Dousing with water would only make the burning process more severe. A nasty weapon indeed. The Serbs used phosphorous in Sarajevo to maximise the killing of civilians and create mini-firestorms setting alight anything in its path. Apparently, dousing with vinegar or urinating on the wound helps reduce the ferocity of the burning action.

Meanwhile, I once again sunk down low into my seat, pulling my flak-jacket tight and fastening my helmet firmly on my head for comfort, trying to make myself as small as possible and not think too much about our current predicament. There was nothing we could do except sit it out and make progress as and when we could. Some of the shells were so near, causing the Land Rover to shake as splinters struck the reassuring Kevlar armoured side panels. It sounded like someone had thrown a handful of gravel at the side of the vehicle whenever the splinters struck. Hans and I exchanged glances of reassurance. Shards of hot metal tore into earth, brick, vehicles and flesh alike, casualties, lay on the ground around us - some crawling trying to find cover with their last remaining ounce of strength. We would be okay as long as we did not suffer a very near or direct hit - I assured myself.

Eventually, our 'cargo' was delivered into the safe hands of the hospital. I was particularly glad to leave the hospital area. Snipers had been shooting through the windows and killing those already injured in the conflict; that is until all beds were moved away from windows. A particularly macabre way to prosecute war; and one didn't get so much as a mention in the press.

The deafness and ringing in my ears from the shelling subsided after a couple of days, but even now, I have to concentrate hard when being spoken to if there is any background noise. I believe this to be a legacy of the warehouse shelling.

That evening, in the privacy of my room, I knelt on the floor next to my bed, reflecting on the day's narrow escape with the Grim

Reaper. Although not a particularly religious person, I clasped my hands together and thanked the Lord, for quite simply, allowing me to live: I was indeed grateful. The close proximity of the shells would I'm sure, make a Christian of the most ardent atheist, or perhaps remove the soul from those already converted. I determined that, if there was a God, he had been watching over me on this day and I needed to make peace with myself - and thank him.

I was emotionally and physically drained and felt as though I didn't belong here any more - this couldn't be reality. I remained kneeling for an hour in a calm and distant trance - from dusk until complete darkness. Only then, in the illusion of safety that only darkness brings, did I crawl, unwashed and fully clothed, into my bed, finally putting the day behind me, preparing myself for the next.

The following day, after sleeping soundly through the nights shelling, I went to the warehouse to inspect the vehicles and building for damage. I wanted to see if the warehouse had been hit in the overnight 'mini-blitz'. I found that the building had not been hit, but there was significant debris and damage in close proximity, indicating to me that, although receiving no direct hits, this wasn't indiscriminate shelling. Our storage facility, for the first time had been directly targeted: an interesting and frightening development.

The truck that was leaking water, was so badly damaged that a repair could not be effectively carried out with the limited resources we had available. Two large pieces of shrapnel that had caused the water to gush out had penetrated the engine cowling and heater matrix. One of the chunks of metal had gone through the air conditioning radiator and embedded itself deeply in the thick metal of the engine block. I dug out the shrapnel with my knife, held it firmly in my hand, and imagined what it would have done to me, had it tore through my flak-jacket and into my stomach, or pierced my helmet and into my skull only the day before. The possibilities of mutilation were in fact endless and didn't really bear thinking about, but I found it so difficult not to. The offending shrapnel had missed me by less than a couple of feet before embedding itself into the guts of the truck. The warehouse wall adjacent to where I was standing at the time of the shelling was severely scarred. The shrapnel struck it at approximately 1,000 mph. I remember standing and thinking in disbelief how incredible it was, that of all those pieces of hot metal flying around, not one hit me.

I began to dwell on it - I should have been killed. Why wasn't I killed? My distorted mind asked. My thoughts began to wander as I imagined the warehouse staff coming to my assistance, had I become another casualty of this war. I pictured myself from above, lying, bleeding to death on the ground, eyes rolling back into my head as I lost consciousness. I completely re-enacted the scenario many times in my head. I imagined the box containing my body being flown out of Sarajevo on a Lockheed C130 transport plane, just like those of the dead Legionnaires, other aid workers, and journalists recently killed. Who would have gone to my room to gather my belongings, to bag them up and send them home, vetting anything that might prove to be insensitive, just as someone had to go through Paul's belongings when he was killed. Who would have visited my parents to tell them of the loss of their son? The son they so readily dismissed all those years before. Who would remain standing next to my grave when others had long gone home? Who would visit and place flowers in the years that followed…

These thoughts slowly matured in my head: I began to feel terribly alone and vulnerable, more so than ever before. My continued living was as much down to luck as anything else: I had been *very* lucky.

This previous day's experience is one that I feel significantly changed my outlook on life and how I now live. Complete exposure to the power of deadly explosive ordinance and flying shrapnel in such close proximity has had a *lasting* effect upon me. The jagged piece of razor sharp metal I held in my hand represented the thin line between survival - and meeting an abrupt and messy end. Shells, designed by well brought up, educated men in white-coats, to fragment into deathly sharp pieces of shrapnel, causing premature termination of the lives of others - it just didn't make sense. None of it did.

After this incident, and in the interest of preserving our valuable vehicles, the remaining three trucks were parked well away from each other, reducing the risk of losing them all to one well-placed salvo of shells. We should have done this before but no one thought that we would ever be targeted directly. A ridiculous oversight in the circumstances. Nothing was beyond destruction in Sarajevo.

I gathered my thoughts and walked on to an old broken down crane that was home to two puppies I had recently adopted and had been taking care of. They were getting fatter by the day with mashed corned beef and milk powder that I had been feeding them. They loved it! I presumed they had been abandoned by their mother or maybe orphaned. I looked under the crane and thought they were asleep. I smiled to myself as I looked down upon them - my puppies. When I touched them, they were both hard and cold. My smile turned to a frown and my eyes quickly filled with tears as I realised they were both dead.

There was no blood or marks on their bodies and they seemed quite serene. I could only presume the noise, shock, or compression of the exploding shells over the previous twenty-four hours had snatched life away from their fragile little bodies. For some minutes, I knelt beside them. Then carefully picked them up, again asking the question that is asked so often in war, 'why?'

With one hand holding the puppies, I took my dirty white helmet off, wiped my brow, then carefully placed my innocent dead little friends inside the helmet and carried them to the nearby railway embankment - where some of the shells had previously landed. Using my helmet, I scraped a hole in the already softened earth and carefully placed their little bodies inside, laying them to rest. I covered them over with the soft earth and said the Lord's Prayer (the only one I knew) then left - deeply saddened. The death of animals strangely affected me more than human suffering. Animals are *always* innocent, taking only what they need to live. Humans take what they want needlessly - including life.

As time went by, I got to know all the soldiers on the various checkpoints surrounding the city, getting pretty used to drinking Slivovitz and Hecegovacka Zoca, both nauseating, locally produced, potentially lethal spirits; my normal non-smoking teetotal, diet-conscious values temporarily suspended for the duration of the war. I would sometimes sit drinking these toxic substances when crossing from Sarajevo into the 'Republic of Srbska'. The soldiers on duty appreciated this even though they initially regarded me with suspicion, as I did them. However, we soon began to regard one another as friends. The effect of the occasional drinking session (which wouldn't amount to more than two or three shots for me) meant that I sometimes traversed confrontation lines in a complete state of carefree oblivion - such was my low tolerance of alcohol. The warehouse staff would laugh and hustle me into Vojo's office, whilst he prepared a dose of thick black sludge masquerading as coffee. Other warehouse staff would park up my truck.

Drinking with the checkpoint guards was, I deemed, a necessary step in ensuring a peaceful co-existence with bored, despondent and trigger happy soldiers. This being satisfactory justification in my mind. It also had the added benefit of stopping them checking my cab, where I hid all sorts of 'forbidden' goods that I would bring back into Sarajevo. This could be whisky for Hans, or nothing more than sausage meat or bread for me. Nevertheless, the checkpoint guards had a habit of confiscating anything that wasn't on the official inventory.

In times of increased hostility, Hans and I were confined to our office, and sat drinking bottles of beer and whisky brought in from the nearby village of Grbavica (it was virtually impossible to obtain such items in Sarajevo). We passed the the time by playing cards and improvised a game of basketball with homemade balls made from paper and tape and a net mounted on the wall. Fortunately, when drunk, we were never needed to complete any tasks, as by 1.00 pm we were invariably asleep in our chairs: empty bottles littered the floor. This seemed an appropriate way to pass the sometimes-endless periods of inactivity, which was often thrust upon us.

Occasionally, Hans and I used to drive around the empty city for something to do - through the burnt out shells of houses and over mountains of rubble - just for fun. In summer, the garage staff occasionally managed to obtain enough food for a barbecue. Sitting outside, whilst eating, we could often watch a minor offensive, by one side or another taking place some two miles away. On reflection, it seemed quite eccentric, even more so when stray rounds would pass overhead or strike the roof of the workshop or garage doors. However, this was a much needed and relaxing way to spend sunny afternoons whilst trapped in the city.

Karl, my colleague, who had the responsibility for water sanitation, became increasingly disillusioned, due to the fact that all his efforts to help provide clean water and sanitation were repeatedly destroyed by either sabotage or shelling.

Karl initially took the destruction of his efforts personally and, much to my amusement would throw a tantrum every time one of his beloved pipes was ruptured. He soon mellowed and, like myself, just accepted that that was the way it was and we were paid either way.

Nevertheless, he eventually became quite depressed and really wondered whether his skills could be better used in Africa, where his work would be more permanent and certainly more appreciated. To cheer himself up, Karl and I would occasionally and somewhat foolishly drive along Sniper Alley at high speed (which was always advisable) just for the thrill of it and to let off steam, knowing full well we could draw fire. We felt largely impervious to bullets in our armoured Land Rover - that is until a round penetrated the Kevlar armour and exited the other side! We weren't as invulnerable to small arms fire as we thought. This promptly put an end to our foolish antic of 'sniper bating'.

We had learned from previous experience that if a bullet struck the Land Rover at an angle, it would probably bounce off. Also, if it hit one of the sloping armoured panels, there was also a good chance it would be deflected. However, if it hit an upright panel squarely, a bullet would almost certainly penetrate. Armour piercing rounds, recently introduced, would penetrate irrespective of the angle that the armour was hit! Neither of us wanted to give up our new found activity but thought it wise not to taunt the Serbian snipers. They only had to be lucky once and would have got us in time.

On another occasion and to relieve our boredom, I foolishly decided to attempt to drive across the river that ran through Sarajevo, at one of its most shallow parts. Karl was with me and he began to laugh as the three ton Land Rover sank into the shale of the riverbed. We became well and truly stuck! His laughter ceased as my efforts in the four-wheel drive Land Rover came to nothing. Even with full differential lock on both axles, the Land Rover refused to budge, merely digging itself further into the fast flowing river. We presented an 'ideal' stationary target to any disgruntled Serbs on the hills above us. Our apparent helplessness and complete vulnerability caused us serious concern. The Serbs were probably laughing and enjoying the entertainment of our ill-fated efforts to extricate ourselves from this potentially serious predicament. Water started to seep through the bottom of the door but fortunately, we weren't shot at and, much to my relief, with legs shaking, managed to reverse the vehicle out of the hole I'd dug - retracing our tracks back to the riverbank and hurriedly exiting the area.

Another incident firmly etched on my memory was when crossing No-Mans-Land, back into Sarajevo, bringing in the first medical supplies for six weeks; I noticed a number of anti-tank mines strewn across the road. This wasn't an uncommon occurrence, but after stopping my truck, mortar shells started to hit burnt out buildings nearby - each one a little closer. My initial thoughts were, 'Why are they targeting those seemingly deserted buildings?' A nanno second later, I realised it was me they were targeting! I was stationary and now a very easy target for an experienced mortar team. Quickly abandoning my truck whilst under fire, I scrambled into the nearby escorting Land Rover, driven by a Belgian Administrator named Bernard. He was fed up of being office bound and wanted to get out of the city. To facilitate this we thought it a good idea if he provided me with an escort - just in case of emergency. This turned out to be an invaluable suggestion.

I distinctly heard small arms fire parting the air around me: it was uncomfortably close. We raced back out of the killing zone to the comparative safety of the near by Serbian lines.

The Serbian checkpoint guards who had just allowed us through, appeared somewhat confused, but nevertheless greeted us. We hastily walked over to the small shack that they used as an office and went inside. Bernard stood next to me as I tried to explain in broken Serbian-English, to a soldier, whom I assumed was in charge what just had happened. He stood staring at me seemingly confused. I took my personal radio from its pouch and informed headquarters, which was only a couple of miles away from our location, then carefully placed it back in its holder. Afterwards, I took out a large unopened bar of chocolate from my bullet-proof vest pocket, sharing it amongst the now gathering soldiers. Some sat at a table and put their feet up, whilst others pocketed the chocolate and lit cigarettes, all seemingly enjoying this unexpected break in their routine. They all expressed gratitude for the chocolate, a surprising treat. The Checkpoint Commander arrived.

The previously relaxed atmosphere changed, as the guards quickly took their feet off the table and stood upright whilst putting out cigarettes. I was then politely 'coerced', by the Serbian Checkpoint Commander, to give a radio interview to the Serbian Press. He saw the propaganda value of the Global Relief Organisation being rescued from No-Mans-Land by the 'glorious Serbian Army', whilst under fire from the 'ungrateful Muslims'. His English was quite good and he made it clear that if no such interview with the local Serbian Army Press was given, we would be held for 'questioning' for some considerable time. He went on to explain it would be in the interests of all if I consented to an interview.

I then sat at the table where the soldiers had been sitting and thought about my situation and chose to not to be unhelpful. Half an hour later, a smiling young woman in her twenties arrived with a microphone, and an old spool-to-spool tape recorder. She was obviously a professional journalist and immediately began to ask me leading questions, in an effort to make me condemn the Bosnian Muslims, which, in the interest of political correctness, I did not. I became very tense. The friendly soldiers had disappeared, leaving me alone with the commander and journalist. I had no idea where Bernard was, but felt sure he was okay. Throughout the interview, I discretely held the mike down on my personal handset, which was safely in its pouch on my waist belt, and broadcast the whole twenty-minute interview, back to HQ. In actual fact this was not such a good idea. In doing so, I tied up our VHF network for the whole of that time. Nevertheless, I wanted the Global Relief Organisation to know what was happening. Apart from that it provided me with some reassurance - knowing that friends were listening. Meanwhile, the Global Relief Organisation HQ had persuaded the Bosnian Muslim Army Commander to order the removal of *his* mines. Forty-five minutes later and after trying to be as evasive as possible regarding questions about the supposed 'amazing rescue by the glorious Serbian Army', the commander decided to stop the interview and allowed us to leave. I found Bernard leaning up against the Land Rover looking pale. I told him briefly about the radio interview - although there was no need. He had heard it on his personal handset also.

We both got back into the Land Rover with Bernard driving, and quickly drove back across No-Mans-Land to recover the truck and supplies. The pressure wasn't over. For a second time mortar rounds zeroed in upon us, along with light machine gun and small arms fire. I quickly exited the Land Rover. Bullets bounced off it's armoured panels as I ran the short distance to my truck. Bernard could not pull directly alongside the truck, as the track was not wide enough to accommodate two vehicles, leaving me exposed. I reached up to the door handle and yanked the door open, half expecting a round to pierce the heavy bullet-proof vest I was wearing and threw myself headlong into the cab then reached back, pulling the heavy Kevlar armoured door shut: much to my satisfaction. The 'enemy' were quite some distance from us. Consequently, their small arms fire was not at all accurate. Mortar fire was however zeroing in with more precision. The explosions were loud, unpredictable, and terrifying. Once again, I had to fight the confusion that ear-splitting close impacting explosions caused, such was the terrific din - even heard inside the truck Although terrified, I knew I wasn't going to panic. I was often afraid, sometimes so much so that I shook with fear but I had never once panicked and wasn't going to do so this time.

Anyone who says they are not scared in situations like this is, in my opinion, lying, mentally unstable, or both. It is *how* you manage fear that's important, and I *would* manage mine. The truck was still intact but, as I was pulling away, I momentarily caught sight of orange tracer rounds approaching rapidly from the left, less than half a mile away. Memorised, I yelled 'Fuck!' at the same time I was deafened by a KA BANG KA BANG! As two large calibre rounds hit my truck. Instinctively, I ducked behind the steering wheel; keeping my foot on the accelerator and nearly driving off the track onto heavily mined ground. One of the large calibre rounds had struck my armoured windscreen; fortunately not penetrating the two-inch thick reinforced glass, but nevertheless, causing considerable fracturing of the screen - and further intensification of my already heightened state of fear. At the same time, another bright high velocity orange ball had flashed in front of my cab - my windscreen would not withstand a second hit. The steering wheel briefly shook and became heavy and began to vibrate.

'Fuck off, - bastards,' I yelled, as I continued to focus on the objective in hand, determined to survive and drive as quickly as possible through the 'killing zone'. This, of course, now depended upon the increasingly accurate mortars, that were falling on the muddy track to the front and sides of me, and whether any more rounds struck my already weakened windscreen.

Stay calm and look hard: there is nearly always a safe resolution to a dangerous situation. Mine was the numerous craters that offered cover from flying shrapnel - should I again abandon the truck if immobilised. I was ready for that. My near side front tyre had been hit, which explained the second ka bang, and temporary loss of steering and vibration through the steering wheel. All the tyres were of military origin and designed to withstand a puncture, having a hard rubber rim to run on. They were intended to 'get you home' in an emergency, even if the rest of the tyre was shot away. I was grateful for that.

The medical supplies were nearly lost as the truck bounced in and out of craters and potholes - in my hurried attempt to drive through No-Mans-Land and out of danger. Bernard had made it through without anything more than the scars of small arms fire, none of which had penetrated the Land Rover's armoured skin.

On reflection, after the incident, I became quietly confident in my ability to handle any dangerous situation effectively whilst under fire.

After completing the remainder of the crossing, and now on a metalled road in Bosnian Muslim territory, I surveyed the damage to my truck, barely noticing the entourage of Global Relief Organisation medical staff, who had been instructed to meet us in the event of either Bernard or myself being injured. Regardless of the people around me I felt entirely alone, reliving the last two hours and, in particular, the last few minutes dashing across hostile territory in the truck: alone but alive. The medical staff and one of our Sarajevan secretaries, who had recently arrived, stood back - giving me the space I needed, but letting me know that they were there. I wasn't injured and did not need them. I took my helmet off, loosened my bullet-proof vest, and wiped the cold nervous sweat from my brow, whilst surveying the damage to the truck. Instinctively, a Belgian colleague came over to me, laid his hand on my shoulder, and asked how I was. 'Fine' I replied coldly, avoiding eye contact, not wishing to show any 'unmanly' emotion. I was fine after all. I was uninjured. Adopting a superficial, casual, 'so what, just goes with the job' demeanour - I was in fact deluding myself - my senses were numbed.

A large amount of the medical supplies had in fact been lost during the dash across No-Mans-Land. The rest looked as though they were just about to fall off the truck and trailer at any time, held on merely by the strength of the sheeting covering it. Escorted by the medical team Land Rover, I cautiously made my way to the warehouse.

The warehouse staff were aware of the incident and had volunteered to stay behind after hours to unload the truck. After parking up, and as I was walking away, I noticed the secretary who had originally come out to meet me standing in my path. Our eyes met but neither of us spoke. She held out her hand and made eye contact with me. I ignored it. On reflection, I now realise how much I needed the comfort she was offering, but chose instead to break eye contact, walk past her, and maintain my charade - betraying my true feelings, shunning any conception of human vulnerability that I was now feeling. I was unable to show any emotion in front of these thoughtful and good people. The concept of showing weakness was something I was not yet familiar with. Another legacy of my childhood? Anyway, they had their own problems to deal with. The job was done: I was alive and that was that.

I knew from the direction of fire that it had almost certainly come from Bosnian Muslim positions. The irony was that the same soldiers fighting for the security of the inhabitants of Sarajevo actually targeted me. The medical supplies I was carrying could in fact save *their* lives.

It soon began to dawn on me that I had probably been used as a political pawn by the Bosnian Muslim Army. By successfully bringing in supplies, I had broke the status quo and effectively - albeit in a small way - the current state of total siege of Sarajevo. My death would have put further political pressure on the United Nations to initiate air strikes on surrounding Serbian positions and hopefully, for the Muslims in Sarajevo, break the siege for good. The Bosnian Muslims in Sarajevo had hoped for this for some time. Naturally, the Bosnian Muslim Army would have denied any involvement in the death of an aid worker, blaming it on the Serbs and vice-versa. In war, human life is cheap, becoming a very poor second to political and military ambitions and objectives.

I heard later that the Serbs had broadcast a heavily edited version of my interview to their people. My interview now condemned the Muslims for placing the mines in the path of an aid vehicle and that I was eternally grateful for being rescued by the Serbian Army. Maybe it was a good idea that I held down the mike key on my radio after all.

The next morning, I awoke early and alone. Once again, I watched the sunrise over the city, bringing with it fresh hope. The sun's rays always cast a bright fresh newness upon the tortured buildings of Sarajevo. That feeling of hope would soon be dispelled by the forthcoming day's events…

I crept down to breakfast to the usual rancid goat's cheese, runny eggs and, if we were lucky, a cob of bread in a varying state of dryness. As the siege progressed the hotel food got worse. The waiters still wore, their ill-fitting formal attire, sagging from their thinning bodies.

I looked around and saw the usual early bird 'vulture' press teams, laughing and discussing where they thought they were going get the best stories that day. I thought to myself, 'They are real war veterans, chasing one conflict after another'. Perhaps their laughter disguised their real fears. The press teams bonded together and looked out for one another. In some ways I envied them, spending so much time together in the same war. I was largely alone and by now beginning to feel it. I began to feel alienated, needing to believe that I had a supportive peer group. It was unusual for me to feel this way, as I normally didn't want to associate with people more than I had to. Today, however, it was different. I needed to know that all was well and above all that it was okay to think the way that I did.

My 'support' came in the way of sarcasm and wit. Other Global Relief Organisation staff came down for breakfast and joked about yesterday's incident.

'Such and Such got hit in exactly the same section of No-Mans-Land as you' A Belgian guy waffled whilst stuffing his face with a mouth full of the dry mouldy bread.

'Ironic, isn't it – should've known it was dangerous'.

'Yes, s'pose so', I nodded in agreement. Jokes were made about how often my vehicles were being hit. I tried to see the funny side of it but somehow just could not.

What I really needed at that time was to reflect upon the previous day's events. Did I do the right thing? Was there anything else I should've done? This time it was different. This time it was a purposeful and *determined* effort to kill me. I shivered and felt as vulnerable as a newborn baby without a mother. However, no realistic support was forthcoming so I stopped thinking about it. There was no satisfactory conclusion that I could draw so I pretended to carry on as normal - whatever normal was. There was no other rational option if I was to stay in Sarajevo.

I was, nevertheless, a little wiser and more aware of my own mental and physical capabilities. Again, my exposure to a near death experience reminded me of how easy it would be to die here in Sarajevo.

One particular Sunday morning, sometime after the incident in No-Mans-Land was all but forgotten, the city was enjoying a quiet period. People had started to venture out of their homes and use the back roads to walk and visit friends and family. I went for a drive around the city in the Land Rover, taking advantage of the undeclared truce.

The French Foreign Legion were busy erecting more anti-sniping barriers in Sniper Alley and, as there was nothing much else happening I, along with a Reuters cameraman and a war correspondent, thought we would watch them - casually parking up nearby.

The cameraman prepared his camera and started to film this inconsequential event - I expect just for something to do. The French soldiers were using old truck container boxes, approximately fifteen feet long and five high, ideal for barricading the streets, to slow up any Serbian attack. More importantly, they blocked the view of snipers who didn't take kindly to their 'game' being obscured from view.

As the large forklift truck manoeuvred the container into position and lowered its forks, two shots rang out. I instinctively took cover behind my vehicle but was unsure from which direction the shots had come from - and if I was on the correct side of my Land Rover to actually be in cover! Quickly, and instinctively, I thought that the sniper must be hidden about one hundred and fifty yards away, the other side of my vehicle out towards the Serbian lines. I peered through the armoured glass of my Land Rover towards where I thought the shots had come from. Behind me, was a large abandoned factory, which I knew was occupied by Bosnian Muslim snipers - I must be right. It was never safe to make an assumption regarding sniper locations, as the city was a labyrinth of passageways and alleys, which were all exposed to the prying eyes of snipers. However, on this occasion I was right.

A disturbing scene unfolded before my eyes. The two shots had penetrated the window of the forklift truck driver's cab but had missed him. As he jumped out, he was struck in the chest by a third round, which cut straight through his bullet-proof vest, punching the life out of him and throwing him backwards onto the ground. I felt ashamed, sick, and disgusted as the Reuters cameraman bent over the young Legionnaire pushing his camera in his face, filming him in his death throes, as his eyes rolled back and blood pumped from his mouth. At that moment I decided that the press weren't the war veterans that I had previously thought but 'career vultures', always on the look out for the next kill. It was a very distressing scene, and one that I often think about even now, selfishly thinking of how easily it could have been me.

The French soldiers reacted quickly and drove an armoured personnel carrier in front of the injured soldier providing him with cover from being shot again, whilst he lay on the ground. They attempted to administer first aid, but it was too late for this twenty-year-old man. Life drained from his body and in seconds he became another needless casualty. I could watch no more and snatched myself away from the scene. I took my helmet off and sat on it, tucked my knees up against my chin, my head in my hands, and propped myself up against the muddied wheel of the Land Rover - distancing myself from reality. I felt sick, helpless and once again alone and vulnerable.

'Shit shit shit, fuckin' shit!' I said repeatedly. Grasping the situation, I consoled myself in my established belief that it *is* okay to die, as long as you are being cared for. He died in the arms of one of his colleagues, covered in blood - being cared for. The filming of the Legionnaires erecting the anti-sniping barrier was not such an inconsequential event as I had thought it would have been.

Within the hour, this soldier's name and film of his tragic death was on all the major news networks, probably before his parents were even aware that their son had been brutally killed.

This incident served to remind me of when in 1993, Croatian forces overran a Muslim village: my convoy of trucks was parked up a short distance away. We dared not get caught up in the advance. A Muslim woman came running towards our parked vehicles, dragging with her what turned out to be her last remaining child of three. She broke down in front of us, shouting and screaming, very quickly becoming the focus of attention of a nearby journalist and his translator. They took great delight in photographing this distressed and impoverished woman. She explained that, after the shelling had stopped, Croatian soldiers broke through Muslim defences and stormed the village. They burnt buildings and shot everyone that hadn't managed to escape. On entering her home, and having just enough time to grab one of her children and hide in a closet she witnessed, through a crack in the door, the execution of her husband. He was ordered to kneel on the floor in front of their other children before being shot in the head. The other two children, who were themselves screaming, were held by their arms struggling as they were also shot.

I understand and empathise with the difficult and important task the press have, but in the case of both incidents, I strongly feel that a little more human understanding would most definitely have not gone amiss. Now, as before, I was sickened but remained detached.

Six months in Sarajevo and my nerves were becoming affected. The war and attrition was most certainly grinding me down. The stress busting trips to Pale had more or less stopped - I missed that. I was developing mild symptoms of shell shock and knew it, a condition identified very early on in World War I, but not officially recognised until two years into the war. I could not stop my left leg from constantly shaking and my left eyelid from twitching. As each week went by, my symptoms became more prevalent - but I didn't seek medical advice. I was in a male dominated environment and had to continue to live up to what I wrongly believed were the expectations of our locally employed staff. However, I had a desperate urge to rid myself of the claustrophobic environment that I was subjected to. Sleeping became more and more difficult and when I did finally manage to sleep, it was light and erratic. My exposure to the events in Sarajevo left me in a heightened state of alert and a feeling of what I can only describe as 'cumulative anxiety'. I began to display a number of other physical symptoms including loss of appetite, exhaustion and irritability, spending more time alone in my room, and not wanting to talk or associate with anyone. Not talking was probably the worst thing I could have done, but I couldn't see it at the time.

I also began to find it increasingly difficult to remain purposeful and maintain a degree of empathy and compassion for the people of Sarajevo. I didn't really care for anyone, except some of the locally employed staff with whom I worked; they remained constantly in my thoughts. They had no escape from this war and its horrors whilst physically I did. Mentally, I wasn't so sure. I continued to see everybody else as a victim waiting to die; in my mind, their future had already been mapped out, so why should I feel or experience any sense of emotion for what were, in fact, the walking dead. Death, for them, surely would be a reasonable escape from the endless suffering, uncertainty, cold, disease, and starvation that they lived with. Surely, death would be better than this. Just a question of when and how, it mattered not. I was also becoming intolerant and resentful of everyone at our HQ, who would ask the impossible and expect the unreasonable. By now, I was becoming totally indifferent to death and human suffering taking place around me and began to question why I was here.

I soon began taking risks that I would not otherwise have taken and in times of apathy believed I was invulnerable; forgetting lessons of survival, that I seemed to be learning over and over again. Maybe it was time I left.

It was obvious to my peers that I was unable to continue for much longer. Hans, my closest friend, had left some weeks before and I now undertook all tasks alone; having no one to share the experience with. I had two weeks left to run on my contract and was determined to honour my obligation. However, it was becoming more difficult to maintain my regular front line hospital visits. Four recent near death experiences within a week had taken its toll on me. I was becoming afraid to go, but knew that the hospital depended on me: I put fear aside. How long would my luck hold out? I asked myself. Was I living on borrowed time, just like the rest of Sarajevo? Was I also waiting for the inevitable? Had my life already been mapped? Was I also a member of the walking dead?

One morning, I was called into the Deputy Head of the assignment's office, and told that I was being sent home with no loss of pay, and would receive a good report, that would be forwarded to the Global Relief Organisation in London.

'You have done more than enough and I am sending you home,' said the Deputy Head. Those very words allowed me to leave with honour. The Global Relief Organisation had made the decision, taking the responsibility away from me. I could leave holding my head up high, now feeling that I had something to live for - the gift of life itself.

Before leaving, I kept the promise I had previously made and loaded up a Land Rover with army ration packs; cramming the small boxes of ready made meals - biscuits, cocoa, sweets and chocolates into *every* available space, and, without the knowledge of my superiors, made my way back to the orphanage I had visited previously. The staff were somewhat bemused by this clandestine delivery. They could not understand why there was no receipt to sign in a country where *everything* had to be signed for.

I never saw the little girl with the red coat; I hope she was able to enjoy some of the chocolate. . .

Chapter Eleven

A dangerous adventure unfolded before my eyes. Danger had become a way of life.

It took two weeks to get out of Sarajevo. Neither the Serbs nor the Bosnian Muslims would grant me safe passage, and issue the necessary documentation allowing me to leave. However, I eventually left with a sense of sadness for the locally employed staff I was leaving behind. The only way out at this time, was to drive to Serbia, and take one of the recently resumed commercial flights out of Belgrade.

Once again, I crossed No-Mans-Land in a Land Rover, wearing two flak-jackets and a helmet, sitting on another flak-jacket with a second helmet protecting my private parts! It really was that dangerous. A couple of days previously, the colleague who had shown concern when my vehicle was hit in No-Mans-Land, had had his Land Rover shot up with twenty or so armour piercing rounds, some incredibly missing him by inches. I was not taking any chances!

I had hidden numerous rolls of photographic film, inside the ballistic panels of one of the flak-jackets that I was wearing. It was strictly against Global Relief Organisation rules to have a camera let alone smuggle out photographs. Should the Serbs have caught me, I would have been arrested as a spy. I made my way, crossing the patchwork of confrontation lines through many destroyed towns and villages, to

Belgrade, the capital of Serbia. There were no visible signs of war in Belgrade, but a lot of resentment towards anyone from the West. United Nations imposed sanctions were crippling their economy. Inflation was running at 300% per day! Britain was an avid supporter of sanctions, so the majority of the Serbian population that I met assumed that I must have supported sanctions too - which I didn't.

After a few days of rest and a couple of trips to the British Embassy in Belgrade to obtain a 'letter of passage', I said my goodbyes and with my driver departed for the airport. Looking forward to the flight to Belgium, I approached customs, safety and good food were just over the horizon. As I was checking in my baggage, customs officials began to rifle through my luggage. I remained calm and patient. A customs officer then asked me how much money I had. I thought this rather unusual, but explained that I had no Serbian Dinars, just English Pounds, and Deutchemarks: some two thousand Deutchemarks - an absolute king's ransom for the average Serb'. The customs officer sharply snapped,

'Show me!' His tone alarmed me. My wallet was promptly snatched from my hand.

'Where have you got this from? You are a Black Marketer! You are spy.' I vehemently denied both of these groundless allegations and started to laugh.

'How long have you been in Serbia?' he barked.

'Four or five days, now grasping the severity of the situation. I then calmly went on to explain that this was part of my salary, accumulated whilst working in Sarajevo. The mention of Sarajevo was a big mistake. I understood enough Serbian to make sense of what he was now saying,

'Only help Muslims in Sarajevo, nothing for Serbs!' Shit, I thought to myself. He's going to blame me for the sanctions next if not the entire fucking war. He gestured to two armed Serb' police officers who were loitering nearby and obviously enjoying the exhibition. They came over and firmly grabbed my arms, whilst muttering something that I didn't understand: I was being arrested!

I continued to protest my innocence and clearly stated I was an employee of the Global Relief Organisation, not a western 'Black Marketer', or spy! At that point, I was discourteously manhandled into a back room by the two thuggish police sidekicks, and forcibly sat behind a desk, whereupon I began to verbally dig myself into a hole.

'Fuckin' 'ell! Give me my money back,' I said. Foolishly holding out my hand expecting him to just hand it back and allow me to go.

'Niet! This is far too much, where have you had it from?'

'I have told you, you thieving commie bastard - I want to make a phone call; I want to ring the Embassy. I want to ring now you thieving git!'

'Niet, niet phone, niet phone,' the customs official steadfastly replied. Obviously, I had totally pissed him off with my disrespect and anger. I guess he wasn't used to that.

'In any civilised country, I would be allowed to make a phone call - I want to ring the British Embassy.' (By now, I had completely lost any sense of composure that I normally demonstrated - but I was so close to going home…). I took out my letter of passage that I had previously collected from the British Embassy and making yet another mistake, waved it in his face. It was in lieu of a visa, and in agreement with the Serb Police Commander at the airport. This was also snatched from my hand - and confiscated. How dare they do this to me? I had diplomatic status but unfortunately, unlike in Bosnia, not diplomatic protection: he could do this to me.

A form was placed in front of me, written in Cyrillic. I was told to sign it, but naturally, not understanding a word of it, I blatantly refused. Apparently, it was to authorise the confiscation of my money. Momentarily, I sat in silence contemplating my fate.

'Sign, sign, sign!' my tormentor kept saying,

'Niet, niet, niet, odjebe!' ('No, no, no, fuck you!') Came my defiant and, in the circumstances, very unwise reply.

To my absolute amazement, he took his pistol from his holster, cocked it, and pressed it firmly against my temple.

'Sign!' he barked - his patience was obviously wearing thin. I turned my head and looked him in the eye with the barrel of his pistol now pressed against my forehead and, in a ridiculous act of defiance, said.

'You won't shoot me, not in front of all these people, you fuckin' prick.' 'All these people', being *his* two colleagues. Once again, I lost my self-control and retaliated the only way, that in the circumstances, I felt I could.

Luckily, for me, I don't think he understood exactly what I was saying. I'm sure from the expression on my face that he had got the general idea all the same. Hand shaking, he replaced his pistol back into its holster. I sat grinning, looking exceptionally smug and somewhat pleased with myself - having won what I felt was a small victory. The room went quiet at which point I began to think how foolish I had been, and not my normal, calm and collected self, but I was thinking of home. I then asked, quite calmly, if my driver, a locally Serbian employed Global Relief Organisation worker, who had seen me arrested, and was waiting at check-in, could come in and translate. The conversation between my captives and myself was flowing far too fast and had left me behind some time ago. He was brought in and promptly urged me to sign the papers. The expression on his face was one of fearful urgency. For a further half an hour, by now having missed my plane, I refused, calmly reasoning that I now had nothing to lose. My driver, a former geography teacher, urged me repeatedly in very good English to sign: telling me that he knew these people and that I *would* disappear, should I not. I certainly had a lot to lose - my liberty.

I asked for the document to be translated and this was duly done. The document authorised the Serb' authorities to hold the money until I could prove where it had been obtained. It was allegedly to be deposited in a government bank. The chances of my recovering the money were, by now, and in view of previous knowledge of Serbian corruption and bureaucracy, nil. I scrawled my signature across the form. From that moment I knew I would never see the money again. It was almost certainly shared amongst the customs officials.

Hostage taking was quite prevalent at that time and I was having visions of an international incident developing. Having missed my flight, and having my paperwork confiscated, I made my way back to the Global Relief Organisation Headquarters in Belgrade with my driver, somewhat disgruntled.

Several days later, and using all the muscle the Global Relief Organisation could muster from the British Embassy, and irrespective of my diplomatic status, I still could not obtain a visa to leave Serbia from the Serbian authorities. The situation became tense, although, at the time, I did not realise the severity of my predicament. Eventually, and together with the head of the Global Relief Organisation Assignment in Belgrade it was decided that I should attempt to leave: taking one of their Land Cruisers. He had good reason to be concerned that I was going to be re-arrested for attempting to smuggle a large sum of money out of Serbia. What was effectively my escape, took me to the northern parts of Serbia, near to the Hungarian border, then swinging westwards towards Croatia, with the aim of crossing into the chaotic and disputed 'Krajina region' and beyond the active front lines, into North Eastern Croatia - and safety.

The journey lasted a tense four days, in which I had to be extremely careful not to navigate myself straight into unfriendly territory. Fortunately, I had an up to date situation map - supplied at a recent intelligence briefing. It was important that I made good progress, as the situation could change dramatically overnight, thus rendering my 'intel' map pretty much useless. However, from this I was able to tell which front lines were active, and work out a route that would help me avoid them and any potential hostile, untrusting militia. They could easily steel my supply of much-valued diesel or take my vehicle, or kill me and have both.

My journey once again took me through many decimated deserted towns and villages that were once front lines. Empty trenches and foxholes, abandoned equipment and the odd corpse - evidence that these places were in a hotly contested region. In order to leave the area unchallenged, I was relying on the fact that communication between the Serbian Army and the Bosnian Serbian Army (operating almost independently of each other but fundamentally on the same side) was not particularly effective.

This lack of communication was something that I could exploit, just in case the Serbs in Belgrade had no intention of ever allowing me to leave and having issued an arrest warrant. They may have wished to use me as a political hostage, possibly discrediting the Global Relief Organisation and the West in general; whilst demanding 'bail' money. They had after all engaged in such practice before. However, on my fourth and final day in Serbian territory, I found that I could not get through the last checkpoint to freedom. This was in spite of me offering two hundred Deutchemarks to the Guard Commander (I had learned the hard way that it was little use trying to bribe the soldiers manning the check point, as I would then have to pay off the commander separately). This was equivalent to six months' wages and such bribes, usually much smaller, had never failed me before. I became concerned.

I radioed the Global Relief Organisation office on the other side of No-Mans-Land and in Croatian territory from my Land Cruiser, informing them of my dilemma. Without hesitation, and as a result of discussion with the local Serbian Commander, and in less than an hour, the Global Relief Organisation arranged for a consignment of various supplies to be delivered to local Serbian refugees, just inside the border of Serbian controlled territory: supplies that were earmarked for other needy people. This alone was sufficient to 'guarantee' my safe passage. I am sure the Global Relief Organisation made good the loss and ensured, as best they could, that the intended recipients got what was due to them. No one, hopefully, went without.

I later learned that two Serbian 'Government Officials' had been sent to arrest me the day after I departed Belgrade. It had been a wise move to leave when I did and probably saved both the Global Relief Organisation and the British Government considerable embarrassment had I been put on trial for smuggling, or any other trumped up charge the Serbian authorities could think of.

The rest of the journey was uneventful. A local Croatian Global Relief Organisation Volunteer, whom I met at the local office, once having crossed into Croatian controlled territory, took over from me and drove the Land Cruiser, whilst I dosed in the passenger seat: happy to relax and be driven.

Passing through the rubble and streets of bombed towns and villages no longer held the visual fascination for me that it once did, having seen it so many times before. Refugees, standing in rags with hands outstretched, hoping for a morsel of food or some clean water were dismissed with an arrogant 'couldn't care less glance' as I was driven by. I did not speak much to the driver, nor did I want to. He sensed that I wasn't in the mood for him to practice his English on me, and anyhow he was young and seemed quite content just driving. I was happy and relieved to have left Serbia, knowing how ugly events could have so easily turned out.

After an overnight stop at a small Global Relief Organisation assignment, in the Krajinas, and a further twelve-hour drive, I arrived in cosmopolitan Zagreb - the capital of Croatia. The war a world away.

The people milling about and the beautiful undamaged Austro-Hungarian architecture awoke my interest in humanity; and to the fact that 'normality' *did* in fact exist after all. Zagreb at this stage of the conflict only ever received the occasional rocket strike, causing little harm and really nothing of any concern - not to me anyway.

I arrived at my hotel at around 9.00 pm. It was the same one that I had stayed in when first arriving in Croatia in 1993. The driver told me to be ready to be picked up at 8.00 am the following morning, on his way to the Global Relief Organisation Headquarters in Zagreb. He quickly disappeared, taking the vehicle back to a secure compound whilst I booked in. I was shown to my room, and as I entered, could smell the clean freshly aired linen. Being too late for an evening meal I sat on the bed and ate a nearly full sachet of American Army ham, (much sought after, and surprisingly the only decent food in their ration packs) it had been opened the day before and saved in my trouser pocket and needed eating - or throwing away. That is to say, it was much sought after in Sarajevo, not here in well-provisioned Zagreb, where there were many 'classy' and expensive restaurants. After eating the ham, I tossed the empty foil wrapper at the bin - and missed. Shortly after, I fell asleep on the bed - still in my grimy sweaty clothes.

I awoke with cramp in my neck after an awkward nights sleep. It was 6.30 am. A hot shower and a change of clothes were in mind. After showering and changing my dirty clothes for some not so dirty ones, (they were last washed by hand in bath water whilst in Sarajevo and smelled a bit musky), I went down to the restaurant and had an enormous and most wonderful breakfast of bacon, eggs, toast and lots and lots of coffee. All freshly prepared. I stuffed food into my hungry mouth and gulped down the delicious coffee between mouthfuls. My lack of table etiquette, (this had never really been a strong point of mine anyway) attracted one or two displeasing looks from more refined clientele; but I really didn't (and still don't) care. I had lost two-stone in weight and was going to enjoy putting it back on!

At 8.00 am, the duty driver duly arrived and took me to the Headquarters, for the first of many debriefings. I wasn't really in the mood for it. Firstly, I contacted Sarajevo via the powerful HF radio to let them know of my safe arrival. During the conversation, I learned that Tanja, the newly wed, had been shot clean through the heart by a sniper whilst queuing for water - she wouldn't have suffered. As predicted, her marriage didn't last...

I wrote a statement about how I thought I was put under undue pressure to make water deliveries to dangerous places, and to travel to unsafe areas. The Debriefing Officer listened, seemingly fascinated, in a professional, empathetic manner. I assumed he had heard it all before and expected nothing to change. I was alive so there was no case to answer.

After that and without much comment, I was asked if I would like to stay and work from Zagreb, as a convoy leader, taking supplies to Bihać, some eighty miles south of Zagreb. I said no but later on in the day and after meeting up with old mates whom I had worked with back in 1993, I reasoned that as I was going to be there for a week or so anyway, I would help.

The following day I embarked on an eight-truck convoy to the 'Bihać pocket'. Not as a convoy leader, but as a regular convoy driver. Bihać, was at that time another Muslim enclave on the verge of being overrun by the Serbian Army.

We met some resistance en-route and were warned by Serbian forces that it was extremely dangerous to proceed. I had previously made deliveries to Bihać whilst working for the UN in 1994 (where the Kenyan troops were previously based) and was surprised that it still hadn't fallen to the Serbs. This was their standard response, as Serbian troops didn't want their enemy supplied with food, or anything else for that matter - which was understandable. We exchanged the usual pleasantries with the Serbs and proceeded anyway. My very last convoy proved well worth the inherent danger of crossing the confrontation line into Bihać. People in the 'pocket' were starving and exceptionally grateful. I remember shedding a tear for them as their bony bodies struggled with the weight of the sacks of flour, as they unloaded the trucks into their warehouse on the outskirts of the town. The tear confirmed to me that I was still able to empathise with the tragedy of war; even after my dismissive attitude towards the refugees', whilst on my way to Zagreb a couple of days earlier.

I determined that this was my last convoy and, after arriving back a couple of days later told the staff of my decision. They accepted this and from my demeanour could see that I just wanted to go home, they applied no further pressure. I was told that if I wanted to come back at any time to let them know. The head of assignment even mentioned that I could come back on a much sought after Belgian contract, which would have been nice, as the pay was considerably more than the British based Global Relief Organisation salary, which in itself wasn't bad.

On the day of my departure, I had my picture taken with all the lads that I had been with on the most recent convoy and some of whom I had known for the last two years. It felt strange knowing I would probably never see them again.

On August 3, 1995, I flew out of Croatia to Brussels, Belgium, for further debriefing and counselling. This was standard practice for all staff returning from the war zone. The gardens at the Headquarters in Brussels were well kept with flowers of many colours. I stared at them, fascinated by their absolute beauty. A startling contrast to the drab, colourless and baron streets of Sarajevo. I wandered around Brussels late into the evening, taking in the sights of what seemed to me to be a beautifully clean city with fast cars and slick restaurants. I was happy with my own company and simply enjoyed watching people go about their business whilst sitting in a high street café, drinking chemically pure coffee made with *clean* water - it tasted awful, and nothing like the bath water coffee I had become accustomed to. I was worried about how I was going to cope with everyday living when I got home.

To watch people laughing, joking, chatting about nothing was for me, a pacifying experience, helping me realise there was a life to be had after my wartime experiences. I could be once again feel safe and free from death. I sat, hoping that I would fit straight back into normality…

Two days later, after the Global Relief Organisation had decided I wasn't mad or any more mentally disturbed than when originally volunteering for service, I flew back home to England arriving at

London's Heathrow Airport. The Global Relief Organisation only ever flies their staff to Heathrow, which was somewhat of an inconvenience for me. Manchester would have been far more suitable.

No one met me at the railway station near home - I wanted it that way. No fuss, just the opportunity to slip back into life quietly. Being at home, alone (I wanted that too) wasn't at all difficult, despite having trouble sleeping. As experienced on previous occasions when returning home, I missed the comforting sound of distant shelling and odd burst of machine gun or rifle fire. I appreciate to many this may sound strange, but if you can hear a shell detonate some distance away then you know it isn't going to kill you. That is somewhat comforting. The one that is not heard is the one that could prove fatal.

I think my family and friends knew me well enough not to have any kind of homecoming celebrations of any type whatsoever. I really didn't want anything like that, as I'm sure I would have felt wholly embarrassed. After being home for a week or so I did in fact give a couple of local newspaper interviews. Despite strongly requesting that they print nothing more than I actually said, I was made into some sort of local hero: this being the last thing I wanted. Following on from that, I gave a couple of interviews to local BBC Radio, giving my version of events and feelings about the war. Just to put the record straight! I enjoyed the live radio interviews. They were quite lengthy, and having little experience with the media, I found them somewhat challenging.

I was determined to enjoy some free time before starting work again and soon went off to Kenya with the girl who interviewed me on the local radio station. We had a superb time but the relationship, as could be expected, didn't last.

When at home and watching news on TV of the latest atrocity that had taken place on the worn out streets of Sarajevo, I once again began to wish I was there. The war wasn't going to let go of my thoughts quite so easily: I was lonely. I began to have difficulty in leaving it behind. I was partly to blame for this, as I would avidly await news bulletins on the war as they occurred, trying to relive the experience; or just not let go.

On August 18th 1995, another high casualty mortar attack in Sarajevo resulted in thirty-seven killed and scores wounded. An attack not dissimilar to the one in which sixty-eight people were killed, and more than two hundred wounded, at the main market in Sarajevo in February 1994; causing world outrage and condemnation at the time. This time there was going to be very serious repercussions for the Serbs. United Nations senior officers had not forgotten the original market place massacre. Both incidents were graphically recorded by television news. Unsurprisingly, there just happened to be a television crew on hand on both occasions.

The future of Sarajevo and in fact the whole of the Former Yugoslavia was ultimately decided as a result of negotiation following the well-scripted atrocities that had taken place. The press were to thank for this.

Expectations were placed upon General Sir Michael Rose, the much-respected British UN Commander, to take a much firmer, confrontational line with the perpetrators of these pointless acts of aggression. Political pressure was brought to bear on all UN commanders to take more severe military action. The West, and in particular the United States, were becoming increasingly impatient with the lack of progress in peace talks, and on August 31 1995, in conjunction with European powers, initiated substantive air strikes in Operation Deliberate Force. This operation, utilising overwhelming UN air power, systematically dismantled Serbian communications, weapon ammunition dumps, and infrastructure, in a devastating well-executed blow. This show of strength and determination by the UN, severely disrupted the ability of the Serbian military and indeed their will to wage war; not only amongst the soldiers surrounding Sarajevo, but throughout the whole Serbian Army.

Prior to this latest attack, all exposed and vulnerable UN ground forces had prudently departed for safer territory, thus denying the Serbian military the option of taking any of them hostage. A lesson learned from previous encounters with the Serbian Army.

Even French heavy artillery located high on Mount Igman joined the fusillade, firing upon Serbian command bunkers, armour, and heavy artillery emplacements. This was most certainly not a gesture as previous pinpoint air strikes had been; but was sufficient to ultimately force an agreement that could, in my opinion, have been made three years earlier, had the UN been prepared to show its teeth - instead of trying to continually reason with the unreasonable.

Operation Deliberate Force finally brought the warring parties to the negotiation table, in an American sponsored peace accord located in Dayton Ohio USA. In the ensuing peace talks, hatred ran hand in hand with 'land grabbing diplomacy' by all the warring factions. However, and despite numerous occasions where the talks were on the verge of complete breakdown, the Former Yugoslavia was carved up to the begrudging satisfaction of the leaders of Croatia, Serbia, and Bosnia.

The key elements of the accord were that Bosnia-Herzegovina would continue to exist within its present and hard won boundaries consisting of two entities. One being the Federation of Bosnia and Herzegovina, which in essence was the Croat-Muslim Federation, having control of 51% of the country and the Serbian Republic recognized as The Republika Srbska which would control the remaining 49%. The central government was to be based in the original capital of Bosnia, Sarajevo, and would be responsible for the overall running of the country. There would be a three-person executive presidency with all parties represented by two elected members from the Croat Muslim Federation and one from the Serb' Republic. Free and fair elections were to be held within nine months of the peace treaty being signed. Refugees would be able to return to their original place of residence and vote. NATO would oversee the transition from war to peace, under the guise of IFOR (Implementation Force) and would guarantee unimpeded access to any location at any time - throughout the whole of the now peaceful territories. Under their mandate, they had the authority to use force if necessary to carry out their duties (unlike the UN, which did not have such authority). A further requirement was that Bosnia, Serbia, and Croatia would cooperate fully with international investigations of war crimes and prosecution of war criminals: at the same time guaranteeing the 'highest levels' of human rights for *all* citizens. In return, trade sanctions would be lifted on Serbia and the arms embargo lifted on Bosnia. This long sought after agreement finally ended the war in the Former Yugoslavia in December 1995.

Despite the presence of the United Nations and the political condemnation of atrocities and genocide that took place, I felt the international community, for the majority of its involvement in the Former Yugoslavia, had no significant effect or real interest in the conduct of the warring parties. That was, until, operation Deliberate Force. Many lives were lost due to the lack of an effective political and military strategy in the Balkans.

It could be argued that the presence of relief agencies, like the Global Relief Organisation and United Nations sponsored organisations, along with international troops, merely prolonged the suffering. Many believe that fate and destiny will decide the outcome of any conflict - a kind of 'let nature take its course' approach. I strongly feel that the armchair warlords, who would so readily write off human life would change their misguided belief, should they have the opportunity to witness first hand the wanton killing that became trademark of this conflict.

Pleas from the Bosnian, Serbian, and Croatian governments, who largely fended for themselves, despite the international relief effort, remained a cry for help which was largely untouched. For many of the innocent victims of the war, the relief effort was nothing more than a *sugar coating* delivered by governments who initially felt obliged to 'do something'. Some would say a kind of official sweetener merely to appease critics. After all, there were no oil supplies to protect - or take control of - in the Former Yugoslavia, nor did her largely under developed economy provide any economical threat to her European neighbours.

Chapter Twelve

And finally...

The shelling has stopped. Snipers have returned home to live with their evil deeds for the rest of their lives - having killed many innocent people. People who no longer have the opportunity of growing old...

War can leave its surviving victims devoid of emotion and afraid of happiness. For some, psychologically, the war isn't over yet. Bodies have been buried and mourned, but evidence of the war will not only remain for decades on the scarred cities, but on the memories of adults and children alike: people don't necessarily have to be hit by bullets or shrapnel to become casualties of war.

Surviving children were robbed of an education, traumatised by the war and siege conditions. I saw them play in silence with grave faces, their eyes deep in thought and sorrow, brutalised by the experience, stripped of their innocence...

War, to those who have witnessed it, is graphic and violent. A shocking and definitive experience. Can anyone find the words to describe the overpowering sense of fear that envelopes someone caught up in a mortar attack, shellfire, or a firefight. The difficulty individuals face maintaining a sense of logic and calm demeanour, when life can be extinguished at any moment is, without doubt, exhausting. The youthful exuberance demonstrated early on in *my* war had completely disappeared.

General Rose, now retired once said.

'You can not expose yourself to that sort of predicament when you are living daily with appalling death and destruction without it affecting you as a human being.' How right he was. Sometimes I turned off my feelings, other times I internalised them. Others I brought home and will live with them for evermore, I hope making me a more caring, thoughtful and understanding person.

A part of me will always remain in the city of Sarajevo, where I lived each day to the full, witnessing the most productive, resourceful, and compassionate side of human behaviour, hand in hand with the most brutal, insensitive, devious, and dark side of the human species. The whole experience making me look at myself in a manner that I would *not* otherwise have done. Indeed, a lifetime compressed into a few short months: a truly rewarding and equally enlightening experience.

Months later, my leg stopped shaking and my eye stopped twitching. Memories of war in the Former Yugoslavia, and later Albania, had a very positive and undeniably worthwhile effect upon me. Those silent memories continue to dominate my thoughts and the way I now feel and experience *everything* I do in life.

Ten years on and despite the efforts of the Implementation Force (IFOR) the Bosnian Serbs, Muslims, and Croatian communities remain resolutely divided - suspended somewhere in-between war and peace. I fear that it will be difficult to maintain an enduring peace in the region once IFOR leaves, should it ever do so.

Every year on the anniversary of Paul's death, I travel to Yorkshire and place flowers on his grave with a simple inscription to let his family know, that I for one, will always remember Paul and his selfless contribution; taking comfort from the words a Padre had once said to me...

'No one is really dead until forgotten.' Paul will *not* be forgotten.

The Price

The conflict claimed the lives of an estimated:

375,000 adults killed
175,000 wounded
51,000 children killed or wounded
More than 1,250,000 people lost their homes

British Special Forces arrested General Galic, the man in direct command of the forces besieging Sarajevo, on December 20th 1999, in his hometown of Banja Luka. He is now facing a war crimes tribunal in The Hague. The unnamed murderer at the water pumping station remains, to my knowledge, a free man.

What Happened to...

Vojo
The last I heard of Vojo, was that he was working for the American Embassy in Sarajevo, having left the Global Relief Organisation. I would dearly like to meet up with him...

Zorren
To the best of my knowledge, continues to live in Italy with his family, hopefully having successfully rebuilt his life.

Hans
Left Sarajevo six weeks before I and returned to continental trucking. I receive the occasional telephone call, when he is in the UK.

'Timmy Tubby'
Also returned to trucking and keeps in touch. Very happily driving across Europe for an international haulier.

Aussie Pete
Continued to work for the Global Relief Organisation throughout the world. I occasionally heard from Pete until he was killed on 20th March 2003 in the Zambia, whilst working for the Global Relief Organisation. He will be sadly missed along with his typical dry Aussie wit'.

John Corbin

Has since worked on a rich Arab Prince's yacht, as a marine mechanic - earning loads and doing very little! I knew he'd make it!

Burt 'the old man'

Turned heavily to drink, after leaving the Global Relief Organisation - and the failure of his marriage. His whereabouts are unknown.

Vince

Now married to his longstanding sweetheart, Molinitta. They have three children. We occasionally keep in touch.

Richard

Now divorced from his wife - Richard built a beautiful new home in windswept Scotland. He is a very devoted father to his three sons - who spend every weekend with him and stay several nights during the week. He is also a successful businessman running two businesses, and makes great effort to keep in touch.

Only the dead see the end of war
Plato

About the Author

John Breardon was born in central England, in 1965. He has a sister Julia and half brother James. Following the early divorce of his parents, he spent time living between them. At the age of ten, after a minor disagreement with his father's new wife, John found himself completely ostracised from family life. His father distanced himself from the situation, offering little support to his only son. He was merely tolerated within the household, fending for himself; cooking, washing, ironing soon became a way of life at this impressionable age. In March 1979, his father gave him an ultimatum that, if he didn't leave voluntarily, he would hire a van and deliver all his belongings to his mother's home. Two days later, John left, knowing to stay would serve no useful purpose, and would in fact jeopardise his father's new marriage.

Now living at his mother's home, the next four years were spent defending himself and protecting his mother against a violent, drunken husband and stepfather. Despite loving his own son James, he physically and mentally tortured his mother, and treated John with utter disregard and contempt. His mother made great effort to provide for her family, which to her credit she did; nevertheless, they lived in near poverty. John resorted to stealing out-of-date cakes and pies from a skip at the local supermarket, where he worked as a Saturday boy. John's older sister Julia, left home and married at the age of eighteen and has since divorced - twice.

As was the case at his father's home, John lived with fear and uncertainty, once again excluded from family life. However, he built strong links with his friends, and, as time went by, came to rely upon the hospitality and generosity of his friends' families.

At the age of seventeen he became homeless. His mother's new husband had finally convinced her that his alcoholism, and violent behaviour, was simply due to John's presence. In fact, the beating and abuse of his mother, had been going on for many years, prior to John's arrival. The mistake in his stepfather's eyes was that John, within days of arriving, had defended his mother against a violent attack: utterly defying him.

John's belongings were packed into black disposable bin bags and left on the pavement outside his 'home'. A short time was spent sharing a locally rented garage with his cherished Honda motorbike, before being offered temporary lodgings by Richard and Edna - dearly loved parents of an ex-girlfriend. A couple of days later, John returned to his mother's house to collect some more belongings. As he approached the front door, he saw his mother through the frosted glass, and heard her fearfully say, 'Oh no it's John, what's he want?' as his drunken angry looking stepfather stood overlooking her from the top of the stairs. Quietly, John walked away, avoiding confrontation, leaving his last few remaining possessions. From that moment on, having virtually no contact or support from his own father, he was entirely alone, and vowed never to look back; or allow himself to ever become so vulnerable again in life.

Richard and Edna looked after him well, helping him find more permanent accommodation in the local YMCA - they had no room to spare. The whole experience made him an extremely determined and indomitable young man.

Soon after, John joined the Royal Engineers Territorial Army, (The British equivalent of the American National Guard). This gave him the structure and identity that he badly needed. It was to provide a useful grounding in discipline, and introduced him to various weapons, and indeed their destructive potential. The military training, combined with schooling and qualifications in combat engineering, a heavy goods driving licence and cross-country driver training, helped rebuild his shattered confidence.

However, a set back was soon to follow. Whilst on a training exercise with the TA in February 1984, John was struck by a speeding car, incurring serious multiple injuries. He awoke semi-conscious, finding himself naked on a cotton sheet draped over what felt like a cold concrete slab. Lifting his head, interrupting the nurse who was standing over him sewing a gash above his left eye, he stared in painless disbelief at a Doctor, screwing a pin through his left leg. In his confused state, he believed he was already dead in a morgue and began to think…

'Well, if I'm going to die, at least I'll die being cared for.' This was the first time in many years that he really felt cared for.

It was a realistic and comforting feeling, as he closed his eyes in a peaceful acceptance of his fate. A welcoming sense of calm settled upon him, as he slipped back into unconsciousness - a safe and serene illusion.

Some time the following day, he awoke to find his left leg suspended in traction, head heavily bandaged, his nerve damaged left arm completely useless by his side; intravenous drips attached to both arms. In disbelief, his father stood at his bedside. Maybe some good had come from the accident. He did care after all…

It was to take more than two years of determination, and painful physiotherapy to recover from the injuries sustained to his head, left arm, and leg.

He was lucky to have professional help almost immediately at hand from his Troop Sergeant, and the British National Health Service. The prompt attention he received was in stark contrast to what he was later to witness in the conflicts that he was soon to participate in, both on the scarred streets and countryside of the war in the Former Yugoslavia, and subsequently the fighting and civil uprising in Albania. Both entirely different kinds of war.

After the degrading experience of youth, an opportunity arose for him to finally establish himself, and achieve some sort of approval and recognition that most young men aspire to. Possibly having more meaning to him, than most people of his age. To accomplish this, he was quite willing, if necessary, to pay with his life.

He joined the Global Relief Organisation in March 1993, and worked as an aid worker, in the war in Bosnia, Croatia, and Serbia, often finding himself in hostile and life threatening environments and leaving an indelible impression upon him. Whilst in Sarajevo, he was the only Global Relief Organisation worker permanently based in the city at that time. He returned home to England in August 1995 after completing his contract, subsequently joining the British Police Force.

In the summer of 1997, he left the police after becoming somewhat disillusioned, and returned to the Global Relief Organisation, this time working in Albania. He has since made several television appearances and given numerous BBC radio interviews on the subject.

To this day, he remains unmarried, and lives in a modest terraced cottage, in a semi-rural part of the United Kingdom.